BISON
BOOKS

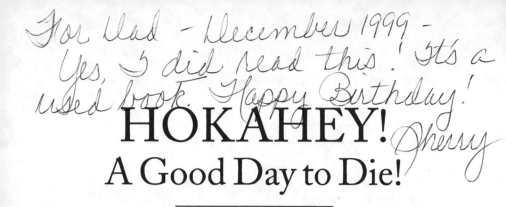

For Dad – December 1999 –
Yes, I did read this! It's a
used book. Happy Birthday!
Sherry

HOKAHEY!
A Good Day to Die!

The Indian Casualties of the Custer Fight

by
RICHARD G. HARDORFF

UNIVERSITY OF NEBRASKA PRESS
LINCOLN AND LONDON

⊗

First Bison Books printing: 1999
Most recent printing indicated by the last digit below:
10   9   8   7   6   5   4   3   2   1

Library of Congress Cataloging-in-Publication Data
Hardorff, Richard G.
Hokahey! A good day to die!: the Indian casualties of the Custer fight / by
Richard G. Hardorff.
    p.   cm.
Includes bibliographical references.
ISBN 0-8032-7322-3 (pbk.: alk. paper)
1. Little Bighorn, Battle of the, Mont., 1876—Casualties.   2. Dakota In-
dians—Wars, 1876—Casualties.   3. Cheyenne Indians—Wars, 1876—
Casualties.   I. Title.
[E83.876.H3   1999]
973.8′2—dc21
99-17520   CIP

Reprinted from the original 1993 edition by the Arthur H. Clark Company,
Spokane WA.

You say that the parents of Lieut. Crittenden loved him, that he was their only child, and that they were sorely grieved at his death. You can judge of the grief and anguish of the parents of the nine young [Indian] *men found by the whites after the battle, lying in the* [funeral] *lodge. They were all brave and good, yes, fine young men, and the grief of the parents is great.*

—Statement by the Hunkpapa, Little Buck Elk at Fort Peck, Montana, September 25, 1876

Contents

Maps and Illustrations

Preface

On a hot Sunday afternoon in June of 1876, hundreds of frenzied Indians converged on a sagebrush-covered ridge rising high above the floor of the Little Bighorn Valley. Scattered along the slopes of this ridge, five troops of the Seventh U.S. Cavalry hastily prepared for a desperate struggle for their lives against an overwhelming force of Indians. The agony did not last very long. After the powder smoke and dust lifted, some 210 troopers lay dead.

News of this tragedy was initially met with shock and disbelief in the East, which soon turned into outrage. Headlines in the newspapers spoke of a massacre perpetrated by Indian savages. Editorials were critical of the War Department and demanded immediate action to revenge this humiliating defeat of a nation then amidst its centennial celebration.

The outrage over this military disaster was in part due to rumors about horrible mutilations inflicted on the slain soldiers. A supporting military column which arrived on the battlefield two days after the engagement was shocked by the carnage. In addition to the mutilations, the exposure to the scorching sun had caused the bodies to swell from trapped gasses, which had pulled the skin taut, making it shine like satin. Decomposition had blackened the bodies, while blow-flies and maggots further hastened the maceration of the remains.

As was the practice among the Plains Indians, families who had lost loved ones at the hands of the whites vented their grief by mutilating the bodies of their enemies. Accordingly, they cut off ears, noses, fingers, limbs and genitals; removed the eyes from the sockets; slashed muscles; broke skulls, or beheaded their white victims; shot the bodies full of arrows and inflicted lance stabbings and gunshot fire on the prone remains.

To the Caucasian mind, such acts were incomprehensible; however, the Indian frame of mind was not inhibited by such restraint. Indian ideology taught not to expect any quarter, and not to give any in return. The mutilation of an enemy body, therefore, was not considered an act of cruelty. Instead, this behavior was the accepted expression of a nomadic warrior culture, to which the Lakotas and Cheyennes belonged.

The pre-reservation High-Plains Indians, being members of a warrior society, lived according to conduct rules designed expressly to perpetuate qualities which made for better warriors. Among these qualities were highly aggressive behavior, strong independence of personal actions, insensitivity to those outside the defined band or tribe, and concepts of property limited only to those within the tribal society itself. Is it any wonder, then, that such egocentric behavior shocked the Caucasian from an agrarian society, which roots came from strong European and puritanical origins?

In a warrior society, where social position depended almost solely on individual warlike actions, highly aggressive behavior became an attention-getting device and a means of status improvement. Used in combination with cultural egocentricity and insensitivity to persons and property outside the band, aggressive behavior approached the heights of virtue in a warrior society. Generally, the more forceful such behavior became, the more attention and increased social status it received from the warrior society itself.

By understanding the behavior of the Lakota and Cheyenne warriors, one will get a better appreciation of some of the acts of aggression and deeds of valor described in this volume. The battle of the Little Bighorn provided the Indians with a wonderful opportunity to display their warrior prowess. Moreover, such exhibitions took place in full view of their families and the entire Lakota Nation. Unfortunately, in some cases their prowess led to foolishness which resulted in tragic endings. This leads us to the purpose of this work.

How many Indian casualties were sustained at the Little Bighorn? Immediately after the battle, military survivors wrote that the Indian loss was very heavy—that the bodies of the dead had "piled up like cordwood," so effective had been the firing of the soldiers. One officer wrote that the Indians had sustained more casualties than the Seventh Cavalry; so the Crow, Curly, had said. No wonder, then, that some estimates have ranged as high as three hundred Indians killed!

Such outrageous estimates indicate a definite lack of understanding of the principles of Indian warfare. Their ideology would not allow large fatality numbers. There is ample evidence, however, that the number of wounded Indians far exceeded the fatalities. This fact probably gave rise to the speculation that many of these wounded died from the trauma of their wounds. The evidence suggests, however, that the opposite was true.

On this very same subject, one knowledgeable white observer commented that the Indian had a remarkable tenacity of life, and that, unless he was shot through the brains, heart or back, there was no certainty at all about his dying. This statement was made by Lt. William P. Clark, acting

Indian agent at Fort Robinson, who added that he had seen many Indians in 1876 who had been shot through the body in different ways, and who were enjoying excellent health a year later.

In this volume I have identified the Sioux as Lakotas, which is the native word for the *Teton Oyate*, the Western Sioux. Lakota is also the term for the language spoken by them. It should be pointed out that the word *Sioux* is considered derogatory among the Lakotas, the name having been derived from an alien language which identified the Lakotas as an enemy nation. The term Lakota has become increasingly popular as a substitute for Sioux in the official native communications. For example, in 1983, the Oglala Sioux Community College changed its name to Oglala Lakota College, and the newspaper serving all Lakota reservations is called appropriately the *Lakota Times*.

During the semi-centennial celebration of the Custer Fight, in 1926, a veteran Minneconjou warrior attended the burial of an unidentified body, thought to have been one of Reno's troopers. After having been told by his interpreter that this dead man was considered a hero among the whites, the old man asked to be heard. He told the assembled crowd that the Indians, too, had suffered casualties—brave men who had fallen on the land upon which the whites were now standing. After a short pause, he added reflectively that the families of these slain men had "cried" for the loss of their sons, brothers, and fathers, and that these slain Indians were also considered heroes among the Lakotas and the Cheyennes.

And heroes they were. This volume attempts to identify these forgotten men and the locations where they were killed while defending their families and a now vanished way of life. This work was made possible through the assistance of many people. I am deeply indebted to them. The following individuals have been especially helpful. Vyrtis Thomas, National Anthropological Archives, Smithsonian Institution, for his assistance in locating materials on many occasions; Emmett D. Chisum, University of Wyoming Heritage Center, for his patience in answering my many requests; Brad Koplowitz, University of Oklahoma Library at Norman, for supplying information about the Walter Campbell Collection; Virginia Lowell Mauck, Indiana University Library, Bloomington, for her assistance in supplying copies of the Walter Mason Camp Collection; Dennis Rowley, Brigham Young University Library, at Provo, for his patience and kindness with which he granted my many and various requests; Hilda Neihardt Petri and the John G. Neihardt Trust for allowing me to quote from the Eagle Elk Interview in *Lakotas Recollections,* and also for allowing me to quote from DeMallie's *The Sixth Grandfather;* and Father Paul S. Manhart, S.J., Holy Rosary Mission, Pine Ridge, South Dakota, for his graceful and kind assistance with the Lakota language, and for putting up with me on those occasions when I thought I knew it all, but should have known better—to all these people I owe a tremendous debt. One more person deserves special mention—my wife Renee, who tolerated my eccentric research behavior and who in so many ways made life a little easier during this time.

RICHARD G. HARDORFF

DeKalb, Illinois

CHAPTER ONE

The Killing of Deeds

Shortly before midnight, Saturday, June 24, 1876, the Seventh Cavalry departed from the Rosebud Valley, determined to cross the Wolf Mountains undetected before dawn. However, as a result of the darkness and delays with the packtrain, the column was unsuccessful in gaining its objective, and it was halted before daybreak, several miles east of the divide.[1]

Early Sunday morning, June 25, the march was resumed. It should be noted that the night march was undertaken to conceal the presence of troops from the Indians. The resumption of the march in broad daylight, therefore, could only jeopardize this very same objective. And that it did, several parties of Indians being sighted near the divide. Of course, these Indians soon learned of the presence of the soldiers from the smoke of careless bivouac fires, while later the billowing dust of the cavalry column left very little to their imagination.

Attempts to intercept these Indians failed, but there is a

---

[1] For an analytical study of this march, see Richard G. Hardorff, "Custer's Trail to Wolf Mountains: A Reevaluation of Evidence," *Custer and His Times, Book Two*, pp. 85-122.

persistent story among the Lakotas that a young boy named Deeds was shot to death by troops, east of the river. The identification of this boy, his tribal affiliation, the kill site, and the circumstances which led to his death, are all matters shrouded by a mass of conflicting information.

As early as 1877, the Military was told by Oglala U.S. Indian Scouts that Custer's troops were discovered by an Indian boy who was herding ponies, and who hastened back to warn the village. This statement is corroborated by two Minneconjou Sioux: Flying By, who, however, spoke of "some" Lakotas who had lost horses, and Standing Bear, who heard a camp crier announce that two men went looking for ponies, and that one of the two was killed.[2]

Additional details of this incident emerge in a 1931 interview with the Hunkpapa, Iron Hawk:

> A boy was out with the party that went hunting and when they were coming back they stopped at Spring Creek. After they got there his horse played out and he was riding home double with someone. Then when he returned, his father told him and another boy to go and get his horse, and that was the last of the boy.[3]

Not only does this statement reveal the purpose, it also discloses the location as being the headwaters of Spring Creek, better known to the whites as the south fork of Reno Creek. Although Iron Hawk refers to them as two young boys, there are other accounts which disagree with this statement. One of these accounts speaks of an old man and his grandson, while another refers to them as father and son.[4]

As a whole, Iron Hawk's recollection is corroborated by

---

[2]Col. Homer W. Wheeler, *Buffalo Days*, p. 178; Kenneth Hammer, *Custer in '76: Walter Camp's Notes on the Custer Fight*, p. 209; Raymond J. DeMallie, *The Sixth Grandfather: Black Elk's Teachings Given to John G. Neihardt*, p. 186.

[3]DeMallie, *The Sixth Grandfather*, p. 190.

[4]*Yellowstone News*, July 1, 1951, clipping in Agnes W. Spring Collection, Univ. of Wyo. Library; White Bull Interview, Walter S. Campbell Collection, Univ. of Okla. Library, Box 105.

the Minneconjou, Iron Hail, who many years later still recalled many of the details:

> On night of June 24, a boy by the name of Thunder Earth came into camp. He had come on foot, having left his horse behind as it was too lame to make it into camp. The next morning, the boy and his father went out after the horse. The cavalry came upon them and killed the boy, but the man escaped. He came into camp, yelling, "Soldiers coming fast. They shot Thunder Earth."[5]

Although Iron Hail knew the boy by the name of Thunder Earth—a translation variant of Noisy Walking—other Lakotas identified the young victim by an array of vastly different names. Walter M. Camp, an unheralded avocational historian, went to great length to determine the correct names of the slain boy and his companion. He eventually learned that they were father and son, belonging to the Sans Arcs, a northern division of the Lakotas. His informants identified the old man by the name of *Ozo Gila*. The English rendition, subject to the interpreter's degree of expertise, was Brown Back, Brown Ass, and Pants. The boy was identified by such names as Plenty Trouble, Business, and Deeds, of which the latter is the proper translation of *Wicohan*, his Lakota name.[6]

In 1928, Walter Campbell became interested in this matter, and from the Hunkpapa, One Bull, he learned that the slain boy was known as Deeds. Unfortunately, Campbell's recorder was not a prolific writer, which makes the following transcription difficult to understand:

> Deeds—1st boy killed, 14 yrs old—Little Bear's son—14-15 Hona's bro's son got away… Deeds hunting horses and killed and then word comes back about noon of Cracker Box—Man from Cherry Creek brought word, nicknamed Brown Back.[7]

---

[5] Francis Y. Peterson, "Dewey Iron Hail," *Frontier Times* (Fall, 1961): 18.

[6] Walter M. Camp Manuscripts, transcript, pp. 239-40, 311, 486, Indiana Univ. Library; White Bull Interview (1932), Campbell Collection, Box 105, Notebook 24.

[7] One Bull Interview, Campbell Collection, Box 104, File 6.

In my estimation, the foregoing note seems to suggest that Brown Back was a nickname for Little Bear, who was the father of Deeds. It also discloses the chronological order of two reported incidents: First, the killing of Deeds, and later, an incident with a cracker box which took place in the rear of Custer's troops. However, I am at a loss when it comes to the identity of "Hona's bro's son."

In a subsequent interview, One Bull appears to correct himself because he indicates that Deeds was Hona's brother.[8] The spelling of *Hona* indicates that the word is *Nakota*, the middle dialect spoken by the Yanktonnais, an eastern division of the Sioux. In Lakota, the dialect of the Tetons, the name would be *Hola*. It consists of two words, namely *ho*, meaning voice, and *la*, derived from *cikala*, which means little or small. The name of Deeds' brother was therefore Little Voice. He was the young boy who rode double with Deeds on June 24, after the latter's pony became lame.

Of more significance in the second interview is One Bull's startling revelation that Deeds was killed on the west side of the Little Bighorn River, on the flat where Reno crossed in retreat.[9] It should be pointed out that others, too, had indicated this location as the site where Deeds was killed. One of these was the Oglala, Eagle Bear, who related:

> Custer first shot and killed an Indian boy who was camped with his father a few miles below our village. The boy was helping his father skin buffalo when the soldiers fired into the camp. The soldiers rode on, but the father jumped on his horse and hurried to warn us.[10]

The reference to a killed buffalo suggests that Eagle Bear's

---

[8] One Bull Interview, Campbell Collection, Box 105, Notebook 19.

[9] Ibid. This interview contains a sketch on which Deeds' kill site is marked on the west side of the river, with the notation, "shot here by sold."

[10] Unidentified newspaper clipping in Spring Collection, Univ. of Wyo.

recollection may have been confused with another incident which took place on the east side of the river. On the same morning that Deeds was seen near the divide, a lone Sioux hunter had killed a buffalo, far up Reno Creek. He had started to skin the animal, when dust clouds rising from Custer's column east of the divide drew his attention. Mistaking the dust for an approaching buffalo herd, he hastened back to the village to organize a communal hunt with the other members of his camp. This hunter, whose name may have been Fast Horn, later learned of his precarious situation near the top of the divide.[11]

Additional evidence relating to Deeds' kill site on the west bank is provided by Joseph G. Masters who went to Standing Rock in 1936 to secure the facts of this case. Wrote Masters:

> After stopping to water the horses as they crossed the river, the [Reno] soldiers rode far out toward the western hills where the Indian boys were herding the horses. In their story of the battle, all of the Indians recounted the fact that the soldiers killed a ten-year-old boy by the name of Deeds, but that his father, Little Bear, who was wounded, and his brother, Hona, both escaped.[12]

As his source, Masters identified Mary Crawler, who was interviewed by Frank Zahn on Masters' behalf shortly before her death. She was known to her own people as Moving Robe Woman, the daughter of Crawler, a leader of a small Hunkpapa band and a member of the Silent Eaters, a distinguished soldier lodge. Zahn was an accomplished interpreter, an educated mixed blood, who had risen to be a judge of the Standing Rock Indian Court of Offenses.[13] There is no reason to doubt Mary Crawler's statements, except her iden-

---

[11]James McLaughlin, *My Friend the Indian*, p. 44; W.A. Graham, *The Custer Myth*, pp. 60, 61; Hammer, *Custer in '76*, p. 84.
[12]Joseph G. Masters, *Shadows Fall Across the Little Horn: Custer's Last Stand*, pp. 30-31.
[13]Ibid., p. 31.

tification of names. In another interview with Crawler, in 1931, conducted also by Zahn, she very clearly states that the name of her slain brother was One Hawk, and that Brown Eagle was the name of the young man who escaped. Perhaps this was her Lakota way to conceal the true names of both individuals.[14]

It should be pointed out that Mary Crawler may have added considerably to the controversy surrounding her relationship to the boy, and also the location of his kill site. According to Ed Lemmon, a respected rancher and longtime resident of South Dakota, Mary Crawler participated in the Custer Fight to avenge the death of her uncle. This relative, she said, was hung from a tree on Lance Creek, a short time before the Custer Battle took place.[15]

This statement contradicts the information given to Charles Eastman, an educated Santee raised among the Hunkpapas, who learned that Mary Crawler's brother was killed in the Rosebud Battle. Indian sources do confirm the killing of a young boy during this fight, but the list of Indian casualties does not include the name of One Hawk, or Deeds.[16]

A thorough examination of the Indian accounts seems to refute that the killing of Deeds took place on the Rosebud. However, some informants place the kill site on the Rosebud side of the divide. In regards to this very matter, Walter Campbell questioned his Hunkpapa sources, resulting in the following published conclusion:

> [Moments before Reno's attack,] Fat Bear dashed up to the council tipi. Brown Back had brought the news, he said. That morning early, two young Hunkpapa boys were out looking for

---

[14]*The Pinedale* (Wyoming) *Roundup*, undated clipping, Spring Collection.
[15]Nelly Snyder Yost, *Boss Cowman: The Recollections of Ed Lemmon*, p. 88.
[16]Charles H. Eastman, "The Story of the Little Big Horn," *Chautauquan* (July, 1900): 511.

stray horses. They crossed a soldier trail, and in it found a lost pack.
Curious to see what they had found, they broke it open. It was full
of hard bread. Hungry as boys will be, they sat down and began to
eat. While they were eating, some soldiers came back on the trail,
saw them, and began to shoot. The soldiers killed Deeds, but
Hona's brother made his getaway![17]

Although this quoted segment is somewhat confusing, it
appears that Deeds was accompanied by Brown Back who
Campbell identifies as Hona's brother. The presence of
Brown Back is confirmed by Floyd S. Maine who was inti-
mately acquainted with the Lakotas, from whom he learned
the following:

Another interesting incident in connection with Custer's last
march was related to me by Mato-Sapo-Najene [sic] (Standing
Black Bear), who, with two other young Dakotas named Deeds
and Brown Back, were sent out on an early morning scouting trip
to the hills toward the east of the upper Sioux camp. They had rid-
den for some miles when they crossed Custer's pack trail and, following it for some distance, they found a box of hardtack which
had been lost from the pack train. They broke open the box and
began eating, while Standing Black Bear stood near filling his
warbag with the bread. It is supposed that one of the troopers
missed the lost pack and was returning over the trail looking for it
when he saw one of the Indians. The trooper shot and killed Deeds
instantly.

Standing Black Bear and Brown Back, seeing that Deeds was
dead, and not knowing how many more soldiers might be in the
party, hastily mounted their ponies and made a dash for the nearest
coulee. Following the low ravines, they returned to their camp with
the news. Deeds was, no doubt, the first casualty of the day, even
though he was killed miles away from the scene of the battle, and
some hours before Custer's troops met their end.[18]

As a whole, the story reported by Maine corroborates that

[17]Stanley Vestal, *Sitting Bull, Champion of the Sioux*, p. 160.
[18]Floyd Shuster Maine, *Lone Eagle...The White Sioux*, pp. 132-33.

of Campbell, the difference being that Deeds was accompanied by two other Lakotas, instead of only one. There are other writers who speak of Deeds and two companions. One of these is David Humphreys Miller whose work, *Custer's Fall*, was by some heralded as the best work ever to represent the Indian side. Nonetheless, Miller's efforts are marred by the lingering doubt about his research methods. This was angrily noted by Walter Campbell who accused Miller of appropriating his research data, to publish it as his own.[19]

Overall, the published information by Campbell and others on the killing of Deeds seems convincing. However, the possibility exists that this incident and its location may have been confused with the particulars of another incident. It should be noted that as many as three different parties of hostiles had been observed around the troops near the divide. We may benefit, therefore, from a critical examination of these three sightings, one of which was by Lieutenant Charles A. Varnum who made his observation from a rocky promontory on the divide:

> We saw one Indian riding a pony and leading another at the end of a long lariat, and some distance behind, an Indian boy on a pony. They were evidently hunting stray stock and were perhaps a mile off toward the Little Big Horn and riding parallel to the ridge we were on. There was a gap in the range to our right and the Crows thought they [the Lakotas] would cross there and soon discover Custer. By this time smoke could be seen in a ravine towards the Rosebud showing where Custer was. The Crows were mad that he lighted fires. Boyer [*sic*] said that White Swan, who seemed to be sort of a leader, wanted us to try and cut him [them] off and kill them where they crossed the range so they would not discover the troops. Boyer, Reynolds and two Crows with myself started off dismounted to do so. After, perhaps, a half mile of hard work through very broken country, where we could see nothing, I heard a call like

---

[19]Campbell to Joseph Balmer, Oct. 16, 1957, Campbell Collection, Box 109.

a crow cawing from the hill and we halted. Our two Crows repeated the imitation, but you could easily see they were talking or signaling, and we started back. I asked Boyer what was the matter, but he did not know. On our return we learned that the Sioux had changed their course away from the pass, but soon after our return they changed again and crossed the ridge. We could see them as they went down the trail towards the command and could then see a long trail of dust, showing Custer was moving but we could not see his column. Before it came in sight, the Sioux stopped suddenly and disappeared, one to the right and one to the left, so we knew that the Sioux had discovered our approach.[20]

Although the two Lakotas had noticed the fresh tracks of Varnum's scouts, the sudden appearance of George Herendeen riding ahead of Custer's column startled them, and they immediately vacated the dangerous location. Herendeen was later told by Michel Bouyer that he, Herendeen, had come to within 150 yards of one of these Indians, an object mistaken by Herendeen for a fleeing deer.[21]

Lt. Varnum's recollection of only *two* Lakotas on the west slope of the divide is corroborated by his scouts. The Ree, Bobtail Bull, had seen two abandoned ponies, also on the west side. However, his attempt to recover the prized objects fell short, because when he got near the location he saw two Sioux leading the ponies away. These same two Lakotas had also been seen by the Crow, White Man Runs Him, who pointed out to General Hugh L. Scott many years later the exact spot from the divide—about one and a half miles due west, near a lone pine. The Ree, Red Star, also mentioned the two Sioux, expressing his concern that they might attempt to ambush some of the Ree messengers. And lastly, and signifi-

[20]Lt. Col. Chas. A. Varnum to W.M. Camp, April 14, 1909, Walter Camp Collection, Brigham Young Univ. Library.

[21]Graham, *The Custer Myth*, pp. 262-63; Robert M. Utley, *The Reno Court of Inquiry: The Chicago Times Account*, p. 237.

cantly, we have the statement by Herendeen who, after startling the two Lakotas, "saw two objects going over the hills in
the direction of the Little Horn."[22]

From the information provided by Lieutenant Varnum
and his scouts, we may draw the following conclusion. Only
two Lakotas—a man and a boy—had ascended the west
slope and crossed the divide. Neither one of these two Lakotas was killed at this location, or for that matter, east of the
divide.

On the same morning that these two Lakotas were seen
near the divide, a party of seven Indians was enroute to Red
Cloud Agency, in present northwestern Nebraska. They had
crossed the divide, and while traveling along the north slope
of Davis Creek, they suddenly sighted the smoke of Custer's
bivouac fires. Realizing their precarious situation, they
immediately sought concealment behind the ridges, somewhere between the divide and Custer's camp on the east slope
below. From the divide, Varnum's scouts had detected the
movements of these hostiles, whose ponies looked "as big as
elephants" reflected against the sky.[23]

In the sequence of unfolding events, a third party of Indians should be introduced at this point. Early in June, Little
Wolf and seven lodges of Cheyennes departed from Red
Cloud Agency in order to join their kinsmen in the summer
activities. By June 24, they had arrived at the Rosebud and
were astonished by the sight of a large body of troops near the
present site of Busby. The Cheyennes immediately retreated
to a safer location, although several scouts remained behind
in the nearby hills to watch the troop movements.[24]

[22]Hammer, *Custer in '76*, p. 194; Graham, *The Custer Myth*, pp. 14-15; Orin G. Libby, *The Arikara Narrative of the Campaign against the Hostile Dakotas*, pp. 91, 93; Graham, *The Custer Myth*, pp. 262-63.

[23]Varnum to Camp, April 14, 1909, Camp Collection, BYU; Libby, *The Arikara Narra-tive*, p. 91; Graham, *The Custer Myth*, pp. 14-15.

The next morning, however, the troops had vanished. After Little Wolf was notified, the small band of forty people commenced to follow the trail of shod tracks and fresh droppings. Somewhere up Davis Creek, three of the Cheyenne outriders—Big Crow, Black Horse, and Medicine Bull— came across a box of hardtack, which diverted their attention. At this precise moment, Sergeant William A. Curtiss made his appearance.[25]

Although most writers assumed that Curtiss was detailed to recover this box, close scrutiny of the evidence refutes this conclusion. A study of the packtrain reveals constant problems with loose packs. This was especially a problem during the night march, which caused the train to string out, making effective control impossible. As a result, instructions were given to abandon any loose cargo which impeded the progress of the train. Consequently, details of both F and M Troops "lost" packs.[26]

Careful examination of the evidence discloses that Sergeant Curtiss sought to recover his "personals" bag, a fact attested to by Captain Myles Moylan at the Reno Court of Inquiry, in 1879. This bag probably contained such articles as an extra pair of woolen socks, a spare shirt, and other items prized highly by a trooper far away from civilization. This bag was not lost during the night march, but was left behind accidentally at the location where the night march had come to a halt.[27]

---

[24]Camp Manuscripts, IU, p. 367; Hammer, *Custer in '76*, p. 214; Thomas B. Marquis, *Wooden Leg: A Warrior Who Fought Custer*, p. 250; Marquis, *Keep the Last Bullet for Yourself*, p. 92; *Billings* (Montana) *Gazette*, May 26, 1927, clipping in Custer Files, Billings Public Library.

[25]Marquis, *Wooden Leg*, p. 250; Camp Manuscripts, IU, pp. 267-68.

[26]John M. Carroll, *The Benteen-Goldin Letters on Custer and his Last Battle*, p. 180; Graham, *The Custer Myth*, pp. 137, 241; Utley, *The Reno Court of Inquiry*, p. 207.

[27]Utley, *the Reno Court of Inquiry*, p. 207.

When Curtiss learned of his loss, he obtained permission to return to this location. In compliance with strict safety regulations, a squad was detailed to accompany him, consisting of Troopers James Rooney, William Brown, Patrick Bruce, and Sebastion Omling. After riding some five miles, this detachment arrived at the vacated camp site and observed several Indians examining the discarded cargo of the packtrain.[28]

The confusion about Sergeant Curtiss' mission was undoubtedly the result of faulty recollections of his contemporaries, who naturally remembered the result of his dispatch, but not its objective. Thus, in many accounts, Curtiss is depicted as recovering boxes of bread, although among the refuse was even a mule's cadaver with its rancid cargo of bacon still attached.[29]

This sudden confrontation with the enemy must have startled Curtiss' men. However, they had the presence of mind to fire several rounds at the Cheyennes, who scattered over the nearby ridges. Subsequently, these three Cheyennes joined the seven Lakotas already on the north ridge of Davis Creek and told them of the incident.[30]

The facts of this brief encounter and its participants are thus quite clear. The Cheyennes and *not* the Sioux were involved in this confrontation, and none of these Cheyennes was killed. It follows logically, therefore, that the young boy named Deeds was not involved in this incident and could not have been slain in the rear of Custer's troops.

We know that none of the seven Lakotas hiding along Davis Creek had been killed. One of them, the Oglala, Owl

---

[28]Walter Camp Notes, BYU, p. 195; Edward C. Baily, "Echoes from Custer's Last Fight," *Military Affairs* (Winter, 1953): 177; Gen. Edward S. Godfrey, "Notes on Chapter XXII of Homer W. Wheeler's 'Buffalo Days'," Roll 9, Study Collection, Custer Battlefield National Monument (hereafter cited as CBNM).

[29]Camp Manuscripts, IU, p. 72.

[30] Marquis, *Wooden Leg,* p. 250; Hammer, *Custer in '76,* p. 203.

Bull, related how the Cheyennes had urged them to return to alarm the village. Although Owl Bull had counselled against such a move, they reluctantly decided to go back. Enroute, they came across the remains of Deeds, the body lying somewhere on the west side of the divide.[31]

After considering all the testimony, it seems certain that Deeds was *not* killed on the east side of the divide. And it is equally certain that neither Sergeant Curtiss, nor his detail, shot the boy. Evidence also refutes the possibility that Deeds was killed at the cracker box site. Although two Indian informants claim that they witnessed this incident, testimony indicates overwhelmingly that Deeds and his companion were alone.

It is possible, of course, that errors in memory and interpretation caused some of these erroneous recollections. As a result of misinterpretation, the informant was thought to have been present with Brown Back and Deeds, and because Deeds was killed quite some distance from the battlefield, the incident was probably correlated later with Sergeant Curtiss' startling experience.

The exact location of Deeds' kill site is not known. Walter Camp was told by a Minneconjou that the boy was slain a short distance below the forks of Reno Creek. This could mean anywhere within five miles of the Little Bighorn, because the informant did not specify whether the lower, or the upper forks.[32] The following evidence, however, seems to suggest that Deeds died near the east bank of the river, as told to Walter Camp by several Minneconjous:

> Hump[ed] Little Crow and others insisted that one of the two men who discovered Custer on A.M. of June 25, was wounded and died in brush near L.B.H.; that they were wounded by soldiers or scouts and tried to get to the village to warn it, but the soldiers fol-

---

[31]Camp Notes, BYU, p. 635; Hammer, *Custer in '76*, pp. 203-04.
[32]Camp Manuscripts, IU, p. 486.

lowed close to them and they ran into brush near the L.B.H., and soldiers got to village first and one of them[Indians] dies.[33]

The identity of Deeds' slayer has never been determined. The Oglala, Low Dog, claimed that some Indian scouts in advance of Custer's troops did the killing. This sentiment was also expressed by Feather Earring, a Minneconjou. He told General Scott that two San Arcs were looking for horses when Reno's scouts killed one of them. We know that the Rees and the Crows had ample opportunity to commit the act. I am convinced that they did, and that one of the Crows was responsible. Many years after the incident took place, one of the Crows recalled that a Sioux had been slain some distance from the battlefield, and that the Crow, Goes Ahead, had done the killing.[34]

Deeds' death was of no consequence to the outcome of the Custer Battle. It seems fitting, however, to point out that the boy gave his life in the attempt to alarm his people. This unselfish act merits the recognition of whites and Indians alike. The story is told among Deeds' relatives that upon learning of his death, Deeds' sister, Mary Crawler, obtained a revolver and fought Custer's soldiers as fiercely as any of the men. She distinguished herself by killing two troopers.[35]

[33]Camp Manuscripts, IU, pp. 90-91.

[34]Graham, *The Custer Myth*, pp. 19, 75, 97.

[35]Masters, *Shadows*, p. 31; Yost, *Boss Cowman*, p. 88.

CHAPTER TWO

The Valley Fight

On Sunday afternoon, June 25, 1876, Major Marcus A. Reno and three troops of cavalry crossed to the west side of the Little Bighorn with orders to engage a band of fleeing Indians. It soon became clear, however, that the Indians were not fleeing, and that the troops had struck a village of enormous size. Major Reno therefore discarded his orders of a vigorous pursuit and, instead, halted his battalion to form a dismounted skirmish line. This line extended some two hundred yards across the valley floor, its right flank resting perpendicular on a dry river bend. Here the battle of the Little Bighorn commenced.

Increasing boldness and firepower by the opposing Indian force soon caused the collapse of this skirmish line, which consequently fell back to the protection of the timber. Reno then decided that the position in the woods was no longer tenable and ordered a "charge" to the bluffs across the river. This disgraceful retreat resulted in the death of thirty-five troopers. The exact Indian loss of Reno's abortive attack has never been determined. The following data represents my findings as to the Indian dead, their names, and their approximate kill sites.

One of the more puzzling matters of the valley fight is the question whether the initial attack resulted in the killing of any noncombatants. The Hunkpapa, Gall, claimed on the tenth anniversary of the battle that Reno had killed his two wives and three young children. Since it was rumored that Gall's dialogue was stimulated by a large purse of money, some caution is warranted in the evaluation of his statement.[1]

Many years later, however, it was learned from a retired officer that Gall may have spoken the truth. This officer, known as Captain Cummings, had married a niece of Sitting Bull, and he was then living near Standing Rock Reservation. Cummings was told by his wife's relatives that Gall had gone to secure his ponies at the opening of the Reno battle. When Gall came back to lead his family to the shelter of the bluffs, he found his wife and child (both singular) shot to death in front of his lodge.[2]

Other sources hint at the complicity of the Ree scouts. According to the Bismarck *Tribune* of July 7, 1876, ten women were found slain in a ravine, "evidently the work of Ree or Crow scouts." And to some extent, the Rees incriminated themselves. Take, for example, the following statement by the Ree, Little Sioux, recorded by Orin Libby:

> With Little Sioux there were Red Star, Strikes Two, and Boy Chief. As they stood there looking across the river they saw at the foot of the ridge (about where they were to cross later) three women and two children coming across the flat, running and hurrying along as best they could, on a slant toward the river. Little

[1]Richard Upton, *Fort Custer on the Big Horn, 1877-1898*, p. 110.
[2]Jesse Brown and A.M. Willard, *The Black Hills Trails*, p. 218; *Sheridan* (Wyoming) *Post*, Supplement, undated clipping, probably Sept. 1903, Spring Collection, Univ. of Wyo.

The Hunkpapa Lakota Gall *(Pizi)* whose family was slain during Reno's advance on the Hunkpapa lodges. The painted rings on the white background displayed on Gall's arms indicate that the wearer had been captured by enemies from whom he was able to escape. This feat was accomplished by Gall in 1867, when he was captured and bayonetted by U.S. soldiers near Ft. Berthold. Miraculously he survived his ordeal and managed to escape. Photo credited to David F. Barry, date unknown. *Courtesy Custer Battlefield National Monument.*

Sioux fired twice at them and so did Red Star. Then all four of the
scouts rode through the timber toward the river to kill them.[3]

Upon reaching the river, these Rees discovered a large
pony herd, which whetted their appetite more than the
prospect of scalps, so said Little Sioux. Perhaps so, but it may
be that the Rees learned that the whites did not like to know
about the killing of women and children, a guilt complex
absent from the Indian's frame of mind.[4]

Maybe the Ree, Bloody Knife, was involved in the slayings. According to Fred Gerard, the former and some other
Rees had gone ahead of Reno's troops to capture ponies.
These scouts had approached the teepees, from where firing
was soon heard, and from where Bloody Knife came with
several Sioux ponies.[5]

Regardless of the identities of the slayers, the fact remains
that George Herendeen had seen the bodies of six women in
a little ravine, the same location where Fred Gerard saw the
Rees. And Herendeen asserted that "our men did not kill any
squaws, but the Indian scouts did." These killings were confirmed by the Hunkpapa, Moving Robe Woman (Mary
Crawler), who confided to Frank Zahn that some women
were also slain during the opening phase of Reno's attack.
And finally, we have the statements of returning Southern
Cheyennes who had participated in the Custer Fight, and
who told their Indian agent that some women and children
had been killed at the outset of the fight.[6]

Is there some truth to these alleged killings of noncombatants? I think so. There is no reason to disbelieve Herendeen.
He was considered a respected individual by all who knew

---

[3]Libby, *The Arikara Narrative*, p. 151.
[4]Ibid.
[5]Utley, *The Reno Court of Inquiry*, pp. 94, 146; Libby, *The Arikara Narrative*, p. 150.
[6]Graham, *The Custer Myth*, p. 260; *The Pinedale Roundup*, undated clipping,
Spring Collection.

him. Although with some reservation, I also believe Gall's statement that his family was killed. In view of all this evidence, therefore, I accept as true the *Tribune* total of ten noncombatant casualties, consisting of the six slain women seen by Herendeen, and the other four probably being children.[7]

Although the Indian Scouts were the first of Reno's battalion to cross the river, they were followed shortly thereafter by one sergeant and ten privates who were detailed to skirmish the brush and timber ahead of the column. Great billows of dust were seen to rise from the powdery valley floor, stirred in motion by a large pony herd driven to the village by two young boys.[8]

Private James Wilber, a member of this detail, later recalled that their advance was as far as the outskirts of the teepees. This statement is not supported by other sources, although Lieutenant George D. Wallace did go on record that the skirmish line was within seventy yards of the nearest teepees. In any event, the soldiers had come close enough to rake the lodges with their firing.[9]

The Hunkpapa, Patriarch Crow, better known as Crow King, later told of a Hunkpapa woman who was shot in the shoulder while standing near him. Her shriek made him realize how close the bullets were coming. A similar observation was made by Moving Robe Woman, who saw a Hunkpapa man killed near his lodge, but did not reveal his identity. Fortunately, the Blackfoot teepees, erected at the southern prong of the Hunkpapa circle, stood on benchland considerably lower than the plain from which the soldiers were shooting. Most of the stray bullets rattled harmlessly against the teepee

[7] *New York Herald,* Sept. 24, 1876, reported that a Cheyenne woman was also killed, fighting against Custer.

[8] Graham, *The Custer Myth,* pp. 241-42; Camp Manuscripts, IU, p. 346.

[9] Hammer, *Custer in '76,* p. 148; Utley, *The Reno Court of Inquiry,* p. 51.

The Hunkpapa Lakota Patriarch Crow *(Kangi Yatapi)*. Known to the whites as Crow King, he led an aggressive assault on Custer after his two brothers, Swift Bear and White Buffalo, were killed during Reno's retreat from the valley floor. Photo taken by David F. Barry shortly after Crow King's surrender at Ft. Bufort in 1881. *Courtesy Custer Battlefield National Monument.*

tops, a fact observed by the eloquent Hunkpapa, Pretty White Buffalo Woman.[10]

After the initial shock of seeing soldiers near the edge of their encampment, the Hunkpapa and Blackfoot Lakotas rallied to assist their defenseless women and children. In an interview with Walter Campbell, the Hunkpapa, One Bull, described the opening phase of the attack on Reno's skirmish line:

> On the morning of the day on which the battle occurred, I went out to look up the horses and round them up and then came back to S[itting] B[ull's] tent. Shortly after that a man came up on horse-back and said that the soldiers were not very far away. I took my rifle and went to the house [lodge], and I was not more than two miles away from the soldiers. I went to the house at the village, and just as I got in, they began firing. I was about 22 or 23 years old then. I came out of the house and got on my horse, and took my mother on with me. SB took my grandmother and sister away with the provisions for them. Then things began to happen. I got on my horse again and started to the soldiers. Just past the place where I started, there was a big hill where the Indians were standing, and I crossed the creek and came up to the Indians. At that time the sol-diers were leaving their horses among the trees and were shooting as fast as they could. I called to the Indians to get off their horses and kneel on the ground and to shoot back and try to scare off the soldiers. All the Indians dismounted and commenced to shoot. In a few minutes, I told the Indians to get on their horses and chase the white men, and we all got on our horses. I had a tomahawk [club] and started to run my horse, leaning way down on the other side so the men could not hit us with their shooting. Before we reached them, the soldiers turned and ran into the timber, and we started to make a return and come back and found we had lost one of the Indians. He was the first man killed. Good Bear Boy was the Indian who fell at the upper villages. When I saw this man fall, I told Looking Elk to turn back and take him from the field. He refused to go and I had to go to the man alone. I found he was shot

---

[10]E.H. Allison to E.S. Ricker, March 7, 1906, Ricker Collection, Nebraska State Hist. Soc.; *The Pinedale Roundup,* Spring Collection; McLaughlin, *My Friend the Indian,* p. 44.

in the back, but was not dead yet. I put him across my horse and took him out. The soldiers were now chasing me from the timbers. Before we reached the hill, they had shot my horse thru the hind leg, and the horse could not run. The Indians commenced shooting again and chased the soldiers back.[11]

In spite of the language deficiencies experienced by the interpreter, One Bull himself was incorrect about the fate of Good Bear Boy. In a subsequent account he clarifies and elaborates on the wounding of this young Hunkpapa:

> Our warriors got their horses and started out to attack Reno's line. I was in the lead, but Sitting Bull came up and took my war club and gave me a shield, praying to *Ate* to keep me from doing something rash. He said to me, "You and Good Bear go up and make peace." Good Bear and I came to within thirty feet of the soldiers when they began to fire at us. Good Bear was shot. I picked him up with one arm and held him that way on my horse. I got so angry at the soldiers that I couldn't make peace. I ran back to the gully with Good Bear on my back. Both of Good Bear's legs had been shot and I could hear his bones rubbing together. When I got to the river where I dropped Good Bear, I hit one man in the face with Good Bear's club and killed three others. After I had brought Good Bear into safety, I rode back and killed another soldier and injured two others.[12]

In saving the life of Good Bear Boy, One Bull performed a deed of valor which was very much cherished among the Plains Indians. One Bull alone had turned back and found Good Bear Boy trying to crawl as well as he could, his left leg having been broken, while the right leg showed only a flesh wound. Tying a rawhide thong around the wounded boy's chest, One Bull dragged him out of the immediate line of firing, and then lifted him on his pony, One Bull walking alongside. Good Bear Boy recovered from his wounds and died a natural death at Standing Rock many years later. It was

---

[11]Interview with One Bull, Campbell Collection, Univ. of Okla., Box 104.

[12]Narrative of One Bull, extract, Campbell Collection, Box 115.

told among the Indians that Good Bear Boy was wounded before any of Reno's men were killed.[13]

The shooting of Good Bear Boy may have been witnessed by the Ree, Young Hawk, who was favorably impressed by the Lakota's pony. Orin Libby related:

> One Dakota charged the soldiers very closely and was shot about sixteen feet from the line. He rode a sorrel horse with a bold face and his tail was tied with a piece of red cloth. When the Dakota fell, his horse kept on coming toward the soldiers, and Young Hawk took the horse.[11]

One of the more prominent casualties was the Hunkpapa, Knife Chief, an older man who was the Camp Crier of Sitting Bull's band. He was in the act of shouting Sitting Bull's commands near the skirmish line when he received a gunshot, fired by a soldier lying behind the bank. The bullet travelled through Knife Chief's body, breaking both arms, and wounding him so severely that he remained lying on the battlefield. The shooting of Knife Chief was witnessed by his young son, Steals Horses, who anxiously awaited the removal of his father's body on a pony travois.[15]

In addition to Good Bear Boy, two other young men—Elk Heart and Long Elk—received gunshots, neither of which were of a serious nature since their names do not appear on the Lakota casualty list. According to the Hunkpapa, Shoots Walking, it was the foolish rashness of the younger boys which led to the death of some and the wounding of many of them:

> Long Elk, Pretty Bear, and Elk Heart were the first three that

---

[13]One Bull Interview, Campbell Collection, Box 104, File 6; Camp Manuscripts, IU, p. 350.

[14]Libby, *The Arikara Narrative*, p. 96.

[15]Turning Hawk Interview, Campbell Collection, Box 105, Notebook 38; Nick Ruleau Interview, Ricker Collection, Roll 5, Tablet 29; John P. Colhoff to Chas. D. Schreideis, April 30, 1943, Spring Collection.

were wounded, and then the Indians began to fight. I was but a young boy and wanted to go with the men to fight, and my mother and sister came and put their arms about me and begged me not to go for fear I would be killed. After I got on my horse they held me back so that when the first battle occurred I did not get thru. Just before that [battle] there had been some of the Crows fighting, and Custer [Gen. George Crook] had fought with them, and two or three men were killed. That was the reason my mother and sister did not want me to go. I finally broke away and came down there, but did not go where Reno was. The younger fellows were wild about the fighting…[16]

The sentiments of Shoots Walking are confirmed by the Oglala, Red Feather, a brother-in-law of Crazy Horse, who expressed his view on the matter as follows:

The Indians in the lead were the younger men [who] didn't have enough experience and were reckless. The older ones held off for safety. The younger men were killed mostly, and they took most of the guns.[17]

Perhaps the most vivid picture of the horrors of warfare was given by the Hunkpapa, Pretty White Buffalo Woman. Among the Hunkpapa Lakotas she was held in high esteem for her intelligence, and also for her eloquence in putting thoughts to expression. An unidentified correspondent wrote down the following passage:

Among the killed were boys of twelve and fourteen, who, in the ardor of young warriorhood, rushed across the river on their ponies and into the thickest of the fight. She mentioned two boys who were wounded; one, a young Achilles, in the heel, and another in the right arm, which was shot off. Both recovered and neither of them are yet twenty, though seven years have passed since they counted their first coups.[18]

---

[16]Waukutimonie's (Shoots Walking) Interview, Campbell Collection, Box 111.

[17]Red Feather Interview, Hugh L. Scott Collection, Smithsonian Institution, Box 4, Item 4525.

[18]Graham, *The Custer Myth*, p. 85.

Although one modern source advances the theory that some of the young casualties were suicides, I personally take very little stock in such statements. Among the old Indian families the most cherished possession was their children, especially the first born males. I do not believe, therefore, that these families would joyfully allow their sons to pledge a suicide vow, and that they then would proudly announce this heroic news to their kinsmen during a festive ceremony. One only has to read about the grief of the Cheyenne, White Bull, when learning of the grave condition of his wounded son. No, these boys were not suicides, but rather, as Big Head Woman said, rash boys whose foolish behavior caused them to throw their lives away.[19]

Not all the casualties incurred by the Indians were young men. The Minneconjou, White Bull, related that an old Lakota named Three Bears was wounded next to him while firing dismounted at Reno's troops, and before any Indian resistance was organized. This may have been the individual spoken of by Moving Robe Woman, who saw him get killed near his teepee from a stray bullet. According to White Bull, this was the very first casualty, the old man succumbing to his wounds four days later.[20]

Others were killed, their names being revealed later in an interview with White Bull, conducted by Walter Campbell:

> Before the soldiers go back to timber, [a] young Sioux, Dog with Horns gets shot, and then the soldiers retreat to timber and Good Bear Boy gets shot in hip, and Lone Bull saves him. Then soldiers reach timber and untie horses and run across the river. But before the soldiers get across the stream, they kill Swift Bear, kill White Bull (no relative of W.B.), and wound Chased by Owls.[21]

---

[19]John Stands in Timber and Margot Liberty, *Cheyenne Memories*, pp. 194-95; Marquis, *Custer on the Little Bighorn*, p. 41.
[20]White Bull Interview (1932), Campbell Collection, Box 105, Notebook 24; DeMallie, *The Sixth Grandfather*, p. 196.
[21]White Bull Interview (1932).

White Bull's recollections are corroborated by his brother, One Bull, who recalled that he had led a party of five brave men—Young Black Moon, White Bull, Swift Bear, Good Bear Boy, and one other Lakota whose name time had erased from his memory. Only One Bull and Good Bear Boy lived through the battle to tell their tale.[22]

There exists, however, some uncertainty as to whether Black Moon was killed, and if so, which one. His name is not included on White Bull's casualty list, an exclusion which seems justified by Black Moon's surrender in 1881. Yet the Oglala, Horned Horse, stated as early as 1877 that Black Moon, a Hunkpapa chief, was killed early in the fighting. This statement is corroborated by One Bull, who recalled that Black Moon was slain near Reno's skirmish line. One Bull identified him as the son of Old Black Moon, a relative of Sitting Bull. We may conclude, therefore, that Young Black Moon was indeed killed, and that it was his father, Old Black Moon, who surrendered his Hunkpapa band at Standing Rock in 1881.[23]

In reference to the valley casualties, White Bull elaborated that Dog with Horns was killed shortly after the fatal wounding of Three Bears. Both of these Minneconjou fatalities occurred at the outset of the valley fight. Later, the body of Dog with Horns was recovered by his brother, Feather Earring, who placed the remains in the shelter of some brush, and then hurried into the battle with Custer's troops to vent his grief through vengeance.[24]

The killing of the Hunkpapas, White Bull and Swift Bear, took place during the frenzied pursuit of Reno's fleeing

---

[22]One Bull Interview, Campbell Collection, Box 105, Notebook 41.

[23]Graham, *The Custer Myth,* p. 74; *Chicago Tribune,* May 26, 1877; One Bull Interview, Campbell Collection, Box 104, File 6. According to White Bull's winter count, Old Black Moon died at Standing Rock in 1888.

[24]Graham, *The Custer Myth,* p. 97.

troopers—a running fight which some Lakotas sarcastically referred to as a buffalo chase. However, the deaths of Swift Bear and White Bull caused quite a stir, because they were the brothers of Crow King, a Hunkpapa band leader and an influential man. This might explain why Crow King himself later took an active part in the Hunkpapa assault on Custer's troops.[25]

In addition to the aforementioned Hunkpapas, a Cheyenne named Roman Nose was also slain, while a Two Kettle Lakota, Chased by Owls, was fatally wounded. The Hunkpapa, Hawk Man, was also killed, his death witnessed by Moving Robe Woman, who saw him fall from his pony while charging at Reno's troopers. All of these casualties occurred on the west side of the river. It was rumored among the Lakotas that all but one, Chased by Owls, were slain by Ree Indians, the hated allies of the soldiers.[26]

Examination of the Ree statements seems to confirm the active part taken by them in the slayings. In 1912, many of the surviving Rees were persuaded by Orin G. Libby to record their recollections of the Custer Battle. One of these Rees, Red Bear, described his encounter with a Sioux, which occurred on the west bank, near the ford across which Reno retreated. This Lakota charged upstream toward him, his upper face painted yellow, while the lower half was painted red. Red Bear shot this man, who fell from his pony, which reared up and then wheeled back. This pony followed Red Bear to the east bank, a dark bay with a white blaze on his forehead, and a string of deer hoofs around its throat which rattled as he swam across.[27]

---

[25]One Bull Interview, Campbell Collection, Box 105, Notebook 19; Graham, *The Custer Myth*, p. 78.

[26]Marquis, *Wooden Leg*, p. 268; White Bull Interview (1932), Campbell Collection; *The Pinedale Roundup*; White Bull Interview (1930), Campbell Collection.

[27]Libby, *The Arikara Narrative*, p. 126.

At about the same time this encounter took place, a group of Crow and Ree Indian Scouts had taken refuge in a grove of timber on the east side of the river, a short distance below the retreat ford. Among them was the Ree, Young Hawk, of whom Libby wrote:

> The Dakotas came closer, one on a grey horse came very close indeed. Young Hawk fired and missed him, then he jumped up and shot again, killing him. The horse had a very handsome bridle with very beautiful trimmings, and after the Dakota was shot and fell, the horse kept circling to the left, probably because he was tied by a lariat to the body of the Dakota. Young Hawk fired twice at the horse and at last killed him... "Some little time after this, the Sioux came closer again and I saw one Sioux coming right toward me, and I drew a fine bead on him and dropped him; then I jumped up and gave the dead call again." While this was going on, several Dakota women rode up and gave the women's yell, urging on the warriors to kill all the Arikara.[28]

From the statements by Young Hawk and Red Bear, one could easily be led to believe that both Rees might have had a hand in the slayings of White Buffalo, Swift Bear, and the Cheyenne, Roman Nose. Although this would neatly tie the slain victims with their killers, there remains a question about the locations. There is no doubt that the slaying reported by Red Bear occurred on the west bank, because the victim's pony followed the Ree across the river. However, the deeds of valor so fondly described by Young Hawk took place on the *east side* of the river, from a grove of trees on the flood plain, just below the retreat crossing.

The contradiction in the kill sites of the two Lakotas and one Cheyenne, raises a question which needs to be answered. Did White Bull err in his recollections? Perhaps so about the slayers, but certainly not about the location. I base this on the

---

[28]Ibid., pp. 100–101.

knowledge that White Bull had gone to a great amount of effort to compile his information.

Another explanation for the contradiction might be that the two casualties reported by Young Hawk did not result in any fatalities. Or, perhaps, Young Hawk embellished on the truth to benefit his own standing. Some of this intentional distortion was observed by Walter M. Camp, who interviewed a number of the Rees several years before Orin G. Libby undertook the same task. Regardless of this, I do not think that Young Hawk had a hand in the killings of either White Bull, Swift Bear, or Roman Nose.[29]

Examination of the evidence does link some of the other Rees with the killings on the *east* side of the river. These Indian casualties resulted from the frenzied ride across the river after the fleeing troopers. Careful examination of the Indian testimony reveals that in nearly all these slayings the Rees were involved, belying careless statements that the Ree Indian Scouts were inclined to be cowardly. Thus, in order to reconstruct a scenario for the Indian dead, it stands to reason to examine the statements by the Rees.

We know that the Rees themselves suffered three casualties. One of these was Bloody knife who was killed near Major Reno's side, just prior to the mad scramble from the timber. However, evidence is not so clear as to where the other two Rees had been killed. One of the surviving Rees, Young Hawk, told Walter Camp that the body of his tribesman, Little Brave, lay near the remains of Isaiah Dorman, on the line of retreat, between the timber and the river. However, this statement is not corroborated by other survivors. It should be noted further that Young Hawk was not sure about Little Brave's kill site, because later he told Camp

---

[29]W.M. Camp to Gen. E.S. Godfrey, Jan. 14, 1918, Edward Settle Godfrey Papers, Library of Congress.

that the body was found to the left of the retreat, near the river. He further added that the remains of the third Ree, Bobtail Bull, was also found near the timber, where the victim was headed off and killed by the Lakotas.[30]

In actuality, Young Hawk's statements may have been subject to mental editing. I base this conclusion on what Young Hawk told his brother Rees at the base camp at Powder River—that the remains of the slain Rees had been subjected to frightful mutilation. In all cases, the bodies had been stripped, slashed and hacked in such a way that the skulls had been broken and all facial features had been obliterated, the exception being Bloody Knife who apparently had been beheaded. Young Hawk further told the other Rees that he could not find the body of Little Brave, which contradicts his statement to Walter Camp.[31]

Examination of the Lakota testimony reveals that the deaths of Little Brave and Bobtail Bull occurred on the east side of the river. This is confirmed by the Ree, Red Bear, who had crossed to the east side where he saw Little Brave some distance downstream from him, to the left of the general line of retreat. Little Brave was wounded by a gunshot to the right shoulder, his pony slowly trotting toward the eastern foothills.[32]

At the same time that Red Bear made this observation, his attention was caught by the sudden appearance of Bobtail Bull's pony, which frantically galloped after a number of retreating troopers. This pony was later found on Reno Hill with all of Bobtail Bull's belongings wrapped in a blanket and still tied to the saddle horn. It was noticed that his pony had

[30]Utley, *The Reno Court of Inquiry*, p. 255; Hammer, *Custer in '76*, p. 192; Camp Manuscripts, IU, p. 467.

[31]Libby, *The Arikara Narrative*, p. 145; George B. Grinnell, *The Fighting Cheyennes*, p. 355.

[32]Libby, *The Arikara Narrative*, pp. 127-28.

fresh blood marks on the saddle, legs and hoofs, revealing the telltale story that its rider had been shot *after* crossing the river. This is corroborated by Young Hawk who provided cover fire for Bobtail Bull near the edge of the woods from which Reno retreated. Young Hawk recalled that Bobtail Bull got across the river a short distance below the retreat crossing, pressed hard by the pursuing hostiles.[33]

From the testimony given heretofore by the Rees, we learn that Bobtail Bull and Little Brave had crossed to the east side, and it is thus very unlikely that either one was killed along Reno's line of retreat, on the west side of the river. We also may infer from these statements that Bobtail Bull was shot while mounted, and was probably killed before Little Brave fell casualty. This agrees with the statement attributed to the Cheyenne, Wooden Leg, who claimed that his tribesman, Whirlwind, had charged a U.S. Indian Scout on the flat east of Reno's crossing, where Whirlwind was shot and fell from his pony, mortally wounded. It was rumored later that this sixteen-year-old boy had acted foolishly, and that he had "thrown his life away" in an act of bravado.[34]

After careful consideration of all the evidence, I have come to the conclusion that Whirlwind's opponent was the Ree, Bobtail Bull. Although Wooden Leg's hearsay statement suggests that Whirlwind's shot killed Bobtail Bull simultaneously, the opposite seems to be true. In 1944, John G. Neihardt interviewed an elderly Oglala at Pine Ridge whose name was Eagle Elk, a cousin of the Oglala, Crazy Horse, whose Minneconjou mothers were related. Eagle Elk told Neihardt:

[33]Ibid., pp. 126-27; Hammer, *Custer in '76*, pp. 184, 189; Libby, *The Arikara Narrative*, pp. 97-98.

[34]Marquis, *Wooden Leg*, p. 224; Marquis, *Custer on the Little Bighorn*, p. 41.

I saw that a bunch of Indians were chasing the soldiers up the creek. It was deep and flooded. The Indians could kill the soldiers as they tried to swim. There were two men who ran away from the rest up the hill. They were singing as they ran away, so we knew they were Indians. I was not doing very much, but was keeping back and watching. The two Indians escaped and ran up the hill. Before they got away, a Sioux rode up to them and was going to attack the Ree. The Ree shot the Sioux and he fell off his horse. After that, a man with long hair and all stripped got right up to him and they were both on the ground, and the Ree and Sioux were shooting at each other. The Ree was shot down and fell.[35]

In this account, Eagle Elk identified the Ree's opponent as a Lakota, instead of a Cheyenne. However, such a minor deviation is only trivial, since nearly seventy years had passed since the occurrence of this incident. Eagle Elk's recollection is corroborated by a pictograph drawn by the Oglala tribal artist, Amos Bad Heart Bull. Based on information provided by Oglala elders, the artist revealed that Bobtail Bull was killed by Lakotas, who surrounded him after his slaying of the Cheyenne, Whirlwind. In my opinion, it seems likely that Whirlwind may have wounded and unhorsed his Ree opponent, after which the latter's pony frantically escaped, the streaks of blood showing his owner's fate. The pictograph shows Bobtail Bull afoot, while sustaining a second gunshot fired by the Lakota, Running Eagle. Bobtail Bull was killed by the Oglala, Young Skunk, who himself was slain later in the fight against Custer.[36]

The second Indian casualty on the east side of the river was probably the renowned Lakota known as Elk Stands Above. He was a member of the Sans Arcs and appears to have been a head soldier of one of the military lodges. The first mention

[35]Richard G. Hardorff, *Lakota Recollections of the Custer Fight: New Sources of Indian-Military History*, pp. 102-03.

[36]Helen A. Blish, *A Pictographic History of the Oglala Sioux*, p. 246; White Bull Interview (1930).

of his slaying was made by Captain J.S. Poland, who was told of this incident by the Blackfoot Lakota, Kill Eagle. Although Poland's report states that Elk Stands Above was killed in front of Reno, the evidence indicates that this Sans Arc leader was killed on the east side of the river, in the foothills near where Reno ascended the bluffs.[37]

To determine the kill site of Elk Stands Above, we have at our disposal a pictograph by Bad Heart Bull, which depicts the killing. The translated text by Helen Blish reveals that the slayer was "a Ree Indian who shot a Sioux and then was killed or struck afterward." The Little Bighorn is shown by a wavy line running south to north, while the killing took place at a knoll situated to the right, or east side of the river. Elk Stands Above is shown to the south side of this knoll, ascending the slope, while a Ree is shown on top, the latter being shot by a Lakota on a ridge to the north. Although Blish does not provide a translation, the Lakota text indicates that the Ree was shot by *Mato Wanartako,* known to the whites as Kicking Bear, the prominent leader of the Ghost Dance religion.[38]

In my opinion, the Ree pictured in the above scenario was Little Brave, whose plight was noticed by Red Bear, and recorded later by Orin Libby:

> Downstream he saw Little Brave, who had already crossed the river, and he noticed that he was wounded under his right shoulder, and the blood was running down in a stream over his white shirt. Little Brave's horse was going in a slow trot toward the ridge, but not upstream toward Red Bear... Little Brave was still riding slowly, and he waved his hand to Red Bear to go slowly also. The Dakotas were above them on the hills, firing down at them.[39]

The last glimpse of Little Brave by Red Bear was that the

---

[37] *New York Herald,* Sept. 24, Oct. 6, 1876.
[38] Blish, *A Pictographic History,* p. 247.
[39] Libby, *The Arikara Narrative,* pp. 126-27.

wounded man was riding straight toward the firing of the Lakotas in the hills. The subsequent shooting of Little Brave, and the resulting mob action of frenzied vengeance on an enemy Indian, was witnessed by the Cheyenne, Wooden Leg:

> Another enemy Indian was behind a little sagebrush knoll and shooting at us. His shots were returned. I and some others went around and got behind him. We dismounted and crept toward him. As we came close up to him he fell. A bullet had hit him. He raised himself up, though, and swung his rifle around toward us. We rushed upon him. I crashed a blow of my rifle barrel upon his head. Others beat him and stabbed him to death.[40]

In the case of the Rees, it is interesting to note that the valorous conduct of one of them was particularly remembered by the Lakotas. According to the Minneconjou, White Bull, a Ree known to them as Buffalo Cloud was responsible for the double slaying of two Lakotas, and that this Ree was killed right after the killing of Elk Stands Above. This notoriety is confirmed by Bad Heart Bull who depicted Buffalo Cloud in one of his pictographs. Supplementary information provided by He Dog, the artist's uncle, reveals that the subject of his nephew's artistic rendition spoke the Lakota language.[41]

The above information confirms my belief that the Ree spoken of as Buffalo Cloud was known among his own people as Little Brave, who, according to his tribesman, Red Bear, spoke a little Lakota. Thus, the "singing" noted by Eagle Elk may have been the taunting by Little Brave of his adversaries, in Lakota.

Although White Bull's recollection tallies well with other Indian sources, he is incorrect in stating that the Sioux caught Little Brave's pony. Evidence proves beyond a shadow

---

[40]Marquis, *Wooden Leg*, p. 224.
[41]White Bull Interview (1930); Blish, *Pictographic History*, p. 212.

of a doubt that the ponies of both Little Brave and Bobtail Bull were identified on Reno Hill by the surviving Rees. However, it may well be true that Bobtail Bull's pony later got away from the hill. The story was told many years later that this little animal, though wounded in several places, had returned all alone to Fort Berthold Indian Reservation in North Dakota, after a journey of some three hundred miles—a feat which permanently cemented his name and that of his owner in the songs and stories of the Arikara People.[42]

If we accept the balance of White Bull's testimony as correct—and there exists no reason why we should not—then Little Brave was responsible for the killing of White Eagle, which took place shortly after crossing the river. This encounter may have resulted in the gunshot wound seen by Red Bear in Little Brave's chest. Additional statements by Eagle Elk strongly suggest that White Eagle's death occurred at about the same time that Bobtail Bull killed the Cheyenne, Whirlwind.[43]

Examination of the Lakota casualties sustained during Reno's retreat reveals that White Eagle was the *only* Oglala killed. According to information given to Walter Camp, White Eagle was slain east of the river, possibly while pursuing the troops on their ascent of the bluffs. His father was quite likely the Oglala, Horned Horse, who later told Lieutenant William Clark that his son was killed early in the fight.[44]

The location of White Eagle's kill site is not known for certain, but it appears to have been near the route taken up the bluffs by the troopers. George Herendeen, who was left behind in the woods, crossed the river an hour later and near-

---

[42]Hammer, *Custer in '76*, pp. 184, 189; Stands in Timber and Liberty, *Cheyenne Memories*, p. 210.

[43]White Bull Interview (1930); Hardorff, *Lakota Recollections*, pp. 110-11.

[44]White Bull Interview (1930); Hammer, *Custer in '76*, p. 267.

ly stumbled over White Eagle's body. On reaching the summit of the bluff, Herendeen told Billy Cross, a mixed-blood Sioux interpreter, that if he wanted a scalp he could find one farther down the slope.[45] In this, however, Herendeen was mistaken. Private John Sivertsen, who was with Herendeen, recalled this same incident many years later:

> A short distance up the hill I came across the body of an Indian. He was lying on his back with a carbine in one hand and a whip in the other. I felt his head and found that he had been scalped, so I suppose he was one of the Crow scouts that had joined us some days before.[46]

Of course, Sivertsen was incorrect in his identification of the dead man's tribal affiliation. And Billy Cross, who investigated the prospect of an easy scalp, came too late, because the trophy was already lifted. Years later, Lieutenant Winfield S. Edgerly recalled that he had seen a wounded trooper on the hill who was badly hurt, but who nonetheless displayed great coolness by exhibiting a scalp which he had just taken.[47]

The body of White Eagle lay within rifle range of Reno's men. In agony over the slaying of his son, his old father, Horned Horse, had gone onto the bluffs to wail about his loss and slash himself in mourning. It was not until twilight, several hours later, that the body was extricated by Walking White Cow, a brother of the victim, who confirmed the scalping.[48]

Of the twelve Indian casualties in the valley fight, as many as six were attributed by the Lakotas to the exploits of the Rees. Considering that these recorded killings were accom-

---

[45]Hammer, *Custer in '76,* p. 225.
[46]Herbert Coffeen, *The Custer Battle Book,* p. 44.
[47]Utley, *The Reno Court of Inquiry,* p. 341.
[48]John F. Finerty, *War-path and Bivouac, or the Conquest of the Sioux,* p. 137; Frank Zahn Interview, Campbell Collection, Box 105, Notebook 32.

plished by only four Rees, one gets a better appreciation of the combat skills and valor exhibited by the Ree Indian Scouts. Moreover, of the ten Rees who fought in the valley, three scouts laid down their lives in the service of the United States of America. These undeniable facts put to shame military personnel who stated that the Rees had fled the valley at the first sound of battle.[49]

By means of simple deduction, we know now that as few as only six Indian fatalities may have been inflicted by Reno's troopers. This does not take in consideration the undetermined number of non-fatal casualties. But even if this number was known, it would not significantly change my opinion about Reno's combat force, which was lacking combat skills in general and marksmanship in particular. This deficiency did not escape the elated Indians, who taunted the troopers at close distance during the retreat to the river.[50]

In order to obtain a balanced view regarding the Indian fatalities, it might be beneficial to briefly review the statements by the whites and their allies about enemy casualties. The very first report came from the Ree, Strikes Two, who claimed the killing of a Lakota before the valley fight commenced. Although this claim is not corroborated, Fred Gerard, the Ree interpreter, later testified that "the firing started with some of our scouts that had left the command, and had gone into a little valley to capture some ponies."[51]

Aroused by the boldness of the Rees, the Lakotas went after them and came upon Reno's skirmish line, which then extended partway across the valley. Sergeant John M. Ryan of M Company recalled that "the Indians tried to cut through the line, but several volleys repulsed their charge and

---

[49]Edgar I. Stewart, *Custer's Luck,* pp. 349-50, contains an excellent treatment of this matter.

[50]Marquis, *Wooden Leg,* p. 221.

[51]Hammer, *Custer in '76,* pp. 183-84; Utley, *The Reno Court of Inquiry,* p. 94.

emptied a number of saddles." This temporarily checked the advance of the Indians; but receiving constant reinforcements, they began to test the strength of the line, which soon fell back under pressure to the timber. Lieutenant Charles C. DeRudio, who witnessed these developments, remembered that "he saw two Indians killed in front of us, and several wounded going back to the village. I saw some on the open line drop off their ponies. Lieutenant [Luther R.] Hare got one."[52]

We know now that the mounted charges resulted in a number of Indian casualties. Among these were Good Bear Boy, Long Elk, Elk Heart, and Knife Chief who all sustained gunshot wounds from which they later recovered. Not so lucky was the boy, Dog with Horns, and Young Black Moon, a respected head soldier, who were both killed.[53]

Major Reno's second skirmish line was established behind the bank of a dry river channel, and although this location was judged to be strategically better, only very little time elapsed before Reno decided to retreat altogether. This decision, hastened by the sudden death of Bloody Knife at Reno's side, resulted in disaster. Becoming a disorganized rout, it lacked any military discipline, and it was called by one of Reno's officers the *Suave Qui Peut* Movement—"everybody for himself," with the Indians rendering a "helping" hand.[54]

During this rout, which sealed Major Reno's reputation, the Indians sustained a number of casualties. One of these was attributed to Private Thomas F. O'Neill, who had been unhorsed shortly after the mad scramble from the timber. While attempting to retreat to the woods, one large Indian

---

[52]Graham, *The Custer Myth*, p. 242; W.A. Graham, *Abstract of the Official Record of Proceedings of the Reno Court of Inquiry*, p. 116.

[53]White Bull Interview (1930); One Bull Interview, Campbell Collection, Box 104, File 6.

[54]John M. Carroll, *The Gibson and Edgerly Narratives*, p. 9.

rode right up to O'Neill from behind, but O'Neill turned around and shot the Indian who slumped on his pony and fell to the ground.[55]

And there were others. A young Oglala boy named Black Elk saw one of his tribesmen charge at a soldier and grab the trooper's reins. However, the undaunted trooper unhorsed the Indian with a revolver shot to the body, a feat this soldier was seen to repeat moments later. It was later thought that Captain Thomas H. French was the individual of Black Elk's recollection; but although Captain French boasted to have killed four of his opponents, he did so with his *rifle*.[56]

An experience similar to the one described by Black Elk— but with a different ending—was recalled by the Two Kettle Lakota, Runs the Enemy, and recorded by Joseph K. Dixon:

> The first thing he saw when he got to Reno's battle line was a horse with a bridle on, with the lines hanging down, and a dead Sioux. We passed a black man in a soldier's uniform, and we had him. He turned on his horse and shot an Indian right through the heart. Then the Indians fired at this man, and riddled his horse with bullets. His horse fell over on his back, and the black man could not get up.[57]

We know that the black man was Isaiah Dorman, a Negro interpreter employed at Fort Rice. Fatally wounded, he was killed by a gunshot to the head, fired by the Hunkpapa, Eagle Robe Woman, in revenge for the slaying of a family member.[58]

Trooper James Wilber of M Company also reported an Indian casualty. Wilber survived the battle, but he never forgot how close he himself had come to being a fatality:

[55]Hammer, *Custer in '76*, p. 107.
[56]DeMallie, *The Sixth Grandfather*, p. 182; Graham, *The Custer Myth*, p. 341.
[57]Joseph K. Dixon, *The Vanishing Race*, p. 173.
[58]Hardorff, *Lakota Recollections*, pp. 101-02.

One big Sioux rode alongside of me as we went along at full gallop and tried to pull me from the saddle. He had been shot in the shoulder, and with every jerk he made at me the blood gushed from the wound and stained my shirt and trousers. He was a determined devil and hung on to me until we almost reached the river.[59]

In addition to the reported killing of an unidentified Indian by Red Bear, we have a statement by Private Henry Petring of G Company who recalled his shooting of an Indian on the east bank of the river:

[I] entered the river to ford across and when part way across saw four or five Indians on the bank ahead of me and very near. One Indian, on a cream colored pony, drew up his gun as if to fire, and I, knowing that I was in great danger and would have to act quickly, drew up my carbine without taking aim and fired, and both the pony and the Indian dropped...I did not look back until I had gone some little distance, and when I did I saw two of the Indians carrying off the one I had shot, and the pony still lay there as if dead.[60]

In reconciling the statements by military personnel, we are confronted with a problem of identification of the reported casualties. In addition, these casualties do not represent the actual totals due to lack of data. However, armed resistance by the retreating troopers was reported to be practically nil. For that reason, I have come to the conclusion that Reno's troopers did not extract a higher toll than was reported by the Indians. The following list, therefore, seems to reflect accurately the Indian fatalities of the valley fight.

---

[59]Coffeen, *The Custer Battle Book,* p. 45.
[60]Hammer, *Custer in '76,* p. 133.

Fatality	Location
Six women and four children	just south of the village
Three Bears, Minneconjou	near Hunkpapa teepees (wounded)
Dog with Horns, Minneconjou	front of first skirmish line
Young Black Moon, Hunkpapa	second skirmish line
Hawk Man, Hunkpapa	between timber and river
White Buffalo, Hunkpapa	between timber and river
Swift Bear, Hunkpapa	between timber and river
Chased by Owls, Two Kettle	between timber and river
Roman Nose, Cheyenne	west bank
Whirlwind, Cheyenne	east bank, near crossing
White Eagle, Oglala	on slope near Reno Hill
Elk Stands Above, Sans Arc	on hillock, north of Reno Hill

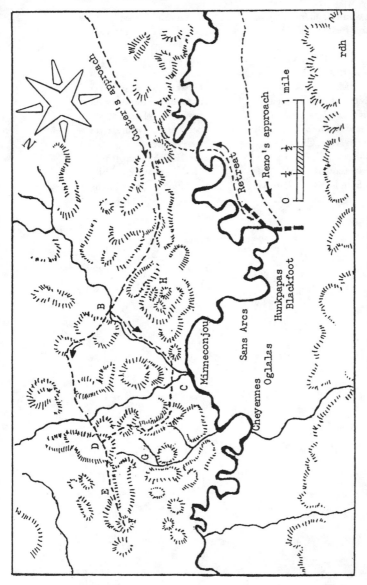

The Little Bighorn Battlefields

A) Reno Hill.   B) Luce Ridge, from where Companies E and F were dispatched to the river.   C) Minneconjou Ford.   D) Calhoun Hill, where members from Companies C and L perished.   E) Location where Company I and surviving members from C and L perished.   F) Custer Hill, the site of the "Last Stand."   G) Deep Ravine, where 28 men were slain on the bottom.   H) Weir Point, farthest point of advance of the Reno-Benteen force.

CHAPTER THREE

The Custer Fight

Before focusing on the Indian casualties, I should briefly set the stage by outlining Custer's route. After dispatching Major Marcus A. Reno in pursuit of the Indians, Lieutenant Colonel George A. Custer and the balance of the regiment followed at a slower pace some distance in the rear. However, instead of crossing the river behind Major Reno, Lieutenant Colonel Custer diverged sharply to the right and ascended Reno Hill. From this elevation, Custer's troopers saw Reno's battalion advancing toward the Indian village.[1]

After going north only a short distance, Custer's column entered Cedar Coulee, which runs north behind the bluffs, and parallel to the river. At the mouth of this coulee, the troops ascended the heights now known as Luce Ridge, from which Captain George W. Yates' battalion was ordered to the river, some one-and-a-half miles west. Custer himself, with Captain Myles W. Keogh, remained on the heights to await the arrival of Captain Frederick W. Benteen's battalion from the rear.

The show of military force by Yates' battalion temporarily

---

[1]This outline is taken from Richard G. Hardorff, *Markers, Artifacts and Indian Testimony: Preliminary Findings on the Custer Battle*.

inhibited Indian aggression near the river. This impasse allowed Custer time to delay his offense, to wait for the eagerly anticipated junction with Captain Benteen. Unfortunately, Benteen's advance was much too slow, and as a result of mounting Indian pressure, Captain Yates' battalion was forced to fall back to present Calhoun Ridge.

With Yates' withdrawal from the river, Custer's position on Luce Ridge was no longer necessary. He therefore ordered Captain Keogh's battalion to advance and join Captain Yates on Calhoun Ridge. At this location, the troops must have realized that the battle to be fought was not for victory, but rather for their own survival. Two days later, the concentration of slain bodies and firing refuse spoke of an anguished tale of desperate resistance.

The sacrifice on Calhoun Ridge enabled the balance of Custer's command to withdraw north to Custer Hill. Further progress was impossible from here, and all came to an end. After most of the officers were disabled, some forty survivors ran for the river to seek shelter in the timber. However, they never reached the river, their decomposing remains being found in a deep ravine, two days later. Thus, the Custer battle ended, and history began.

Of the three phases of the Little Bighorn Battle, none is more difficult to reconstruct than the phase known as "Custer's Last Stand." The same holds true for the study of Indian casualties, particularly in regards to their names and the location of their kill sites. In both cases, we are confronted with a lack of sufficient data.

To a large extent, this problem may be attributed to the statements by the Indian combatants. It should be noted that their frame of mind differs psychologically from that of the whites. Indian recollections are basically recountings of personal incidents which rarely present an overall view. Based on a series of impressions, these statements reflect only that

which the narrator had experienced. Moreover, Indian recollections often lacked references to time and place and therefore lacked cohesion. With this in mind, and considering the
size of the combat arena, one can understand the difficulty
encountered in identifying sites at which Indian casualties
took place.

In 1878, Lieutenant J.W. Pope visited Custer's battlefield
as a member of General Nelson A. Miles' staff. Accompany-
ing the troops were a number of former Oglala and Brule
hostiles who now had enlisted as U.S. Indian Scouts. From
them Lieutenant Pope learned that the troops stationed on
Calhoun Ridge fought a gallant fight, and that nearly all the
Indian casualties in the Custer battle occurred at this location.[2]

A similar observation about the fierce fight at Calhoun
Ridge was made by the Hunkpapa, Gall. Standing at this
very location in 1886, Gall explained that eleven Indians had
fallen casualty on Reno Creek. This drainage, presently
known as Deep Coulee, skirts the base of Calhoun Ridge on
the south side.[3]

Gall's statement is one of the very few sources which provide us with a casualty total. Most other informants are silent
on this point, and what very little we do know about Indian
casualties at Calhoun Ridge, we owe to the field research
conducted by John G. Neihardt. In 1944, Neihardt interviewed an elderly Oglala named Eagle Elk, who related the
following observations of the fight:

> We nine went down and saw the soldiers on the ridge. Before
> we crossed the water we were the first to make a charge. One man
> went out of the bunch and took away the flag that one soldier had.
> The Cheyenne was shot through the heels and his horse stumbled

---

[2]Graham, *The Custer Myth*, p. 115; John M. Carroll, *A Seventh Cavalry Scrapbook, #10*,
pp. 12-13.

[3]*St. Paul Pioneer Press*, July 18, 1886.

and broke his legs. We went right up to the soldiers. Just at this moment we noticed that the other Indians were charging from the south end. From that time the others were coming across the creek after the soldiers. The soldiers were shooting a lot, so the Indians were thrown back. I saw a yellow spotted horse running and no man on him. Just then I saw an Indian running who was shot through the jaw and was all bloody. My brother saw him and came up and helped him, and then we went on chasing the soldiers. I had a brother with me, and as we made a charge, they shot back very heavily so we swung back. Just then my brother's horse was running and he was not on him. I thought he was shot off, and just at that moment there were four soldiers' horses running. I chased after them. I was chasing the horses and got two of them and gave them to another Indian. At that moment I saw a horse shot through the head near the ear. He did not drop, but went around and around. An Indian came and said, "Your cousin is shot off his horse. He is lying over there." But I did not go to look for him. Another man said, "There is a man shot through the head." I found him and saw the man. He wore a bird on his head, and the bullet went through the bird and his head.[4]

This episode reveals the fury of battle on the south slope of Calhoun Ridge. It is significant in that it accounts for possibly four of the eleven Indian dead at this location. Eagle Elk's recollection is corroborated by the Minneconjou, Standing Bear, who was interviewed by John G. Neihardt in 1931. After crossing at the mouth of Medicine Tail Coulee, known to the Lakota as Muskrat Creek, Standing Bear describes the carnage on Calhoun Ridge:

> When we crossed the Little Big Horn you could see nothing but Indians swarming on Custer and you could hear guns going [off] repeatedly. There was a Sioux coming back with his mouth full of blood and his horse wounded, with blood all over him. This was a brave warrior by the name of Long Elk. This is the first thing I saw as [we] were going up there. My party was on the west side of Custer at this time. There were some Indians ahead of us (the fron-

[4]Hardorff, *Lakota Recollections*, pp. 104-05.

ters—all the braves are in the front). I caught a horse and tied it up. As we went on I saw another Sioux with blood in his mouth. He was dizzy. He stood up and then began to come down again—he was wounded. I went on further and saw a soldier lying dead, and there were Indians lying among them on this hill. I don't know how they got killed together, because I wasn't down there.[5]

The Minneconjou Lakota identified here as Long elk was a combat veteran. His name should not be confused with the Hunkpapa boy wounded in the valley fight. Miraculously, Long Elk survived the trauma of his injury, because his name is not among the Lakota dead. The man shot in the jaw was probably not so lucky. He may have been the same individual seen by the Cheyenne, Wooden Leg, while going around Calhoun Ridge to the east. Many years later , Wooden Leg still vividly recalled the horrifying sight:

I saw one Sioux walking slowly toward the gulch, going away from where were the soldiers. He wabbled [sic] dizzily as he moved along. He fell down, got up, fell down again, got up again. As he passed near to where I was, I saw that his whole lower jaw was shot away. The sight of him made me sick. I had to vomit.[6]

Not all the casualties were inflicted by Custer's soldiers. Some of the Indians had shot their own people, mistaking them for Ree or Crow Indian scouts seen with Reno's troops in the valley. At least one such incident took place on Calhoun Ridge. Reflecting on these accidental killings, the Blackfoot Lakota, Kill Eagle, told the Military in 1876 that the Cheyennes had killed a Sioux, mistaking him for a scout from the agencies.[7]

Kill Eagle's statement is corroborated by the Cheyenne, Wooden Leg, who identified the unfortunate victim as a Hunkpapa. He clarified further that the killing was not done

[5]DeMallie, *The Sixth Grandfather*, p. 185.
[6]Marquis, *Wooden Leg*, p. 234.
[7]*New York Herald*, Oct. 6, 1876.

by a Cheyenne, but rather by an Arapahoe and a Santee who repeatedly speared the Hunkpapa's prone body, mistaking it for a Crow or a Shoshone.[8] Left Hand, one of the six Arapahoes who fought at the Little Bighorn, later admitted to the accidental homicide. He had crossed the river at Medicine Tail Ford and saw soldiers on Calhoun Ridge:

> There was lots of shooting all around, and the Indians were all yelling. Everyone was excited. I saw an Indian on foot, who was wounded in the leg…I rode at him, striking him in the chest with a long lance which went clear through him. He fell over a pile of dead soldiers. Afterwards I learned he was a Sioux.[9]

The fall of Calhoun Ridge was inevitable. Speculation continues, however, about the duration of this fight. Two days after the battle, surviving military personnel discovered numerous piles of expended cartridges between the slain. At some locations on the ridge, the count was as many as thirty casings, indicating to the survivors that a desperate fight had taken place.[10] One of the few glimpses of the final moments was provided by the Minneconjou, Standing Bear, who witnessed the resistance on the east end of the ridge:

> When I got far enough over [the rise] to see well, I noticed that the men were off their horses, holding them by the bridles. They were ready for us, of course, and then they began to shoot and the bullets were just raining. The Indians were creeping up to them and the bullets went over us. All of us yelled "Hokahey!" and started charging up the hill. The next thing I saw was soldiers sitting with their hats off on this hill. Then the soldiers immediately started to shoot at us.[11]

After Calhoun Ridge was overrun, the jubilant Indian force surged north along the ridge which now bears Custer's

[8]Marquis, *Wooden Leg*, p. 247.
[9]Graham, *The Custer Myth*, p. 111.
[10]Graham, *Abstract of the Official Record*, pp. 32, 76.
[11]DeMallie, *The Sixth Grandfather*, pp. 185-86.

name. Standing Bear's narrative mentions this movement, with the additional revelation "that Custer was now on a ridge and we followed the ridge there…" Of course, the reference to Custer did not mean Custer himself, but rather his troops.[12]

Of significance in Standing Bear's narrative is the lack of reference to any soldiers fighting in the valley east of Custer Ridge. The lack of such confirmation suggests to me that very little time had lapsed between the annihilation of Troop I and the fall of Calhoun Ridge.

Halfway down Custer Ridge, one will find the unmarked site where a brave Hunkpapa died. The shooting of this individual, Bear with Horns, is confirmed by Standing Bear, who witnessed the incident. Apparently, Bear with Horns had charged from near the head of Deep Ravine at a soldier on Custer Ridge. During the ensuing firing exchange, the Hunkpapa sustained a fatal gunshot before reaching the top.[13]

A few hundred yards farther north is the kill site of one of the seven slain Cheyennes. This man's body was found on the west slope of Custer Ridge, just below the crest, lying face down. Standing Bear and others saw this man, and mistaking the body for that of a Ree, he was scalped by Little Crow, a brother of the Minneconjou leader Hump. Later it was learned that the slain man was a respected individual, known to the Sioux by his Lakota name, Bearded Man. Among his own people, however, he was called Lame White Man, an influential leader, and by birth a Southern Cheyenne.[14]

The death of Lame White Man is mentioned in a number of Indian accounts. Only a few, however, detail the incident. According to the Cheyenne, Wooden Leg, Lame White

[12]Ibid., p. 186.
[13]Ibid.
[14]Ibid.; White Bull Interview (1930).

Lame White Man (sitting) and Old Wolf. This photograph was taken in November of 1873, when a delegation of eleven Northern Cheyenne leaders went to Washington to protest the intended removal of their people to Oklahoma. Although a Southern Cheyenne by birth (c. 1839), Lame White Man married into the Northern Cheyenne tribe and eventually became one of their chosen representatives. He was a proud man who was defiant of the ways of the whites until the very end. He died three years later on Custer Ridge from a gunshot through the chest. *Courtesy of the National Anthropological Archives, Smithsonian Institution.*

Man was killed near the upper reaches of Deep Ravine, while leading a charge against the Grey Horse Troop, which was Company E. This statement is refuted by other Cheyennes.[15]

I might as well state at this point that some skepticism is warranted of Wooden Leg's recollections, as recorded by his biographer, Thomas B. Marquis. There is growing evidence that some of the observations attributed to Wooden Leg came in reality from other sources. This indicates a faulty historical method, and there is also the strong possibility that the recollections contain a lot more of Marquis than one is led to believe. In fact, Marquis, in his desire to prove his suicide theory, ignored contrary statements given to him by these very same Cheyennes. Of course, Marquis' contributions to our store of knowledge far outweighs the flaws mentioned.[16]

In regards to the opening phase of the Custer battle, Walter M. Camp was told by the Cheyenne, Little Wolf, that only *one* skirmish line was deployed by the soldiers, which rested on Calhoun Ridge. Lame White Man had charged this line there and drove part of it along Custer Ridge, to "Keogh," where he was killed. Captain Myles W. Keogh was in command of Troop I, and it is inferred, therefore, that Camp's reference to him denotes the final position of Keogh's troop, across from which, somewhere along the west slope, Lame White Man was slain[17]

Little Wolf's statement is corroborated by the Arapahoe, Waterman. Referring to Lame White Man, Waterman recalled that "Cripple Man, a Cheyenne chief, was killed in one of the first charges made on the soldiers stationed on high ground." A map, purportedly drawn by the Cheyenne, Young Two Moons, supports this contention, as it shows

[15]Marquis, *Wooden Leg*, pp. 241-42.
[16]Ibid., p. 233; Marquis, *Keep the Last Bullet for Yourself*.
[17]Camp Manuscripts, IU, p. 632.

Lame White Man moving from the south end of Custer Ridge to the north.[18]

The manner of Lame White Man's death is known. Referring to him as Walking White Man, Willis Rowland, a mixed-blood interpreter, learned from his mother's people that Lame White Man had charged into the midst of troopers while the fight was raging, and that he fell headlong from his pony after being shot. Similar statements were made by the Sioux. According to the Oglala, Fears Nothing, the Cheyenne dashed right through the soldiers near Custer Hill and was killed.[19]

This reckless charge by the Cheyenne leader was confirmed by the Minneconjou, White Bull, who was astonished and then appalled by the apparent senseless act. This shocking incident was sealed forever in White Bull's mind. Half a century later, he told his friend, Walter Campbell, that this was the only time that he had ever seen a man "throw his life away."[20]

After the battle, Lame White Man's remains were identified by the Cheyenne, Yellow Hair, an older brother of Wooden Leg. The naked body was found partially hidden under some brush. Examination of the remains revealed a gunshot wound in the right breast, the bullet having exited from the back. The scalplock was removed, and the trunk showed additional mutilation from repeated stabbings.[21]

About 1916, a grandson of Lame White Man, John Stands in Timber, was shown the kill site of his grandfather by Cheyenne elders. This site was then marked by a small

---

[18]Graham, *The Custer Myth,* p. 110; Two Moon Interview, Campbell Collection, Univ. of Okla., Box 105, Notebook 15.

[19]*Billings* (Montana) *Gazette,* May 26, 1927; Respects (Fears) Nothing Interview, Ricker Collection, Nebraska State Hist. Soc.

[20]White Bull Interview, Campbell Collection, Box 105, Notebook 5.

[21]Marquis, *Wooden Leg,* p. 242; White Bull Interview (1930); Stands in Timber and Liberty, *Cheyenne Memories,* p. 203.

pile of stones in accordance with a time-honored custom. In 1956, the National Park Service placed an interpretive marker at this site, the sign simply stating that Lame White Man had been slain near there.[22]

After the fall of Calhoun Ridge, the frenzied Indian force surged over Troop I, and then converged on the soldiers remaining on Last Stand Hill. Military observers who later visited the east side of Custer Ridge were critical of the strategy and combat skills displayed on this part of the battlefield. Some merely stated that the troops had panicked, and that they did not fight very well. Others, among whom was the veteran soldier, Captain Frederick W. Benteen, were harsher in their criticism. They called this fight nothing but a rout of Custer's troops.[23]

One of those who agreed with Captain Benteen's evaluation was Lieutenant John G. Bourke who visited the field in 1877, in company of a number of former hostiles who now had been enlisted as U.S. Indian Scouts. After listening to their statements and viewing the field, Bourke arrived at the conclusion that the only effective fight was done at Calhoun Ridge. But after its fall, the surviving troopers ran "like frightened deer" to Custer Hill, so Bourke concluded.[24]

Contemporary Indian statements corroborate Bourke's conclusion. Commenting on the disorder among the troops east of Custer Ridge, the Oglala, Foolish Elk, stated that those soldiers fortunate to be mounted, did not stop to fight, but instead galloped madly to Custer Hill. Left in the rear were the men on foot, shooting their revolvers as they went

---

[22]John Stands in Timber Interview, Aug. 8, 1956, Manuscripts Collection, Research Files, Custer Battlefield National Monument (hereafter cited as CBNM); Stands in Timber and Liberty, *Cheyenne Memories*, p. 203.

[23]Camp Manuscripts, IU, p. 108, statement by Lt. Luther R. Hare; Graham, *Abstract of the Official Record*, p. 145.

[24]John G. Bourke, Diaries, Vol. 21, pp. 65-66, 69-70, U.S. Military Academy Library, West Point.

along, defending themselves as best they could. Through all this chaos, the Indians were exhibiting their prowess by making bravery runs, engaging the soldiers in hand-to-hand combat in the whirling dust and powder smoke. One Lakota said it all when he compared this fight with a grand buffalo chase.[25]

The combat activities on the east side of Custer Ridge resulted in several casualties. We may assume that the unfortunate Lakota described by Wooden Leg did not survive the trauma of his facial wound. He probably sustained this injury near the final location of Troop I. It was also alleged that one of the Cheyennes was killed here. Don Ricky, Custer Battlefield historian, was told by John Stands in Timber in 1956, that the Cheyenne, Long Roach, was slain on the east side of Custer Ridge, near I and F companies.[26]

Unfortunately, the name Long Roach does not appear on any of the casualty rolls, and Stands in Timber himself does not repeat this name on any of his subsequent lists. It is quite possible, therefore, that Stands in Timber was confused with Roman Nose, whose father's name was Long Roach. Be that as it may, the Cheyenne, Roman Nose, also identified as Crooked Nose and Hump Nose, was slain on the west side of the river, during the valley fight.[27]

One of the centers of attraction on Custer's battlefield is an elevation known as Last Stand Hill. After arriving on the top, the visitor finds an unpretentious monument which tells of the armed confrontation that took place on this hallowed ground. Although the monument used to be surrounded by an iron fence, there was room enough on the level hill to view the shaft on all four sides. To the west of the monument is a

[25]Hammer, *Custer in '76*, p. 199; White Bull Interview (1930); Dixon, *The Vanishing Race*, p. 176.

[26]John Stands in Timber Interview, CBNM.

[27]Stands in Timber, *Cheyenne Memories*, p. 204.

level area where the crowd inevitably gathers to view the terrain below. After taking in the sights, the visitor returns to the parking lot behind the monument. He then resumes his sightseeing trip along Custer Ridge, over a blacktop road wide enough to accommodate oncoming traffic.[28]

The geological features of these landmarks were quite different in 1876. Custer Ridge was then a hogback, its length interrupted by several hillocks, its narrow summit not even wide enough to accommodate a wagon. The northwestern end of Custer Ridge terminated in a knoll. Rising six feet above the adjacent ridge, the slanted top of this elevation was some thirty feet in diameter. On the very top of this little knoll, now the site of the present monument, Lieutenant Colonel George A. Custer and nine of his men perished. It was on the backside of this knoll, on its northern slope, that the Indians sustained three fatal casualties.[29]

During the fighting around Custer Hill, two young Cheyennes became reckless, and were consequently killed in separate incidents. Very little is known of them, and their names and kill sites would probably have been forgotten, if not for their tribesman, Wooden Leg. According to the latter, these two young boys were slain on the steep slope just northeast of the monument. He identified them as Black Bear and Limber Bones, known among the Sioux by their respective Lakota names of Young Bear and Flying By.[30]

In addition to the two Cheyennes, the Lakotas also sustained a casualty on the north slope of Last Stand Hill. The name of the slain individual is no longer known, but since he wore a feathered bonnet, he was probably a combat veteran, an older man who must have been a respected member of his

---

[28]The iron fence around the monument was placed in 1884; the fence around the Last Stand area was placed sometime before 1920; and the blacktop road was laid in 1934. See Hardorff, *Markers, Artifacts and Indian Testimony*, pp. 2, 7.

[29]Hardorff, *The Custer Battle Casualties: Burials, Exhumations, and Reinterments*, pp. 33-34.

[30]Marquis, *Wooden Leg*, pp. 268-69. The Lakota names were determined by cross-checking the Lakota and Cheyenne rosters in the appendix.

tribal community. The death of this Lakota is described by Wooden Leg:

> A Sioux wearing a warbonnet was lying down behind a clump of sagebrush on the hillside only a short distance north of where now is the big stone having the iron fence around it. He was about half the length of my lariat rope up ahead of me. Many other Indians were near him. Some boys were mingled among them, to get in quickly for making coup blows on any dead soldiers they might find. A Cheyenne boy was lying down right behind the warbonnet Sioux. The Sioux was peeping up and firing a rifle from time to time. At one of these times a soldier bullet hit him exactly in the middle of the forehead. His arms and legs jumped in spasms for a few moments, then he died.[31]

Although Thomas B. Marquis narrated this incident as seen through the eyes of Wooden Leg, there exists doubt whether the latter actually witnessed the killing. In 1928, Marquis interviewed an elderly Cheyenne named Big Beaver for three days on Custer Battlefield. Present during the interviews was Joe Blummer, the owner of a general store at Garryowen. Blummer left a condensed record of Big Beaver's statements, of which the following is an extract:

> He [Big Beaver] says all the Indians from this end of camp went north along the river, thence to the right or east and came up towards Custer from the north side. When he got there he left his pony back some distance and crawled up the coulee just north and a little to the east of where the present monument is here. He described a Sioux with a warbonnet as being just ahead of him. This Sioux would jump up and shoot towards the soldiers on the hill where the monument is, then he would fall down and reload and crawl ahead again. He did this several times. Big Beaver said he was close behind him when he jumped up to shoot again when a bullet struck him in the forehead.[32]

There is little doubt that the Cheyenne boy in the quoted

---

[31]Marquis, *Wooden Leg*, p. 236.
[32]"Big Beaver's Story of the Custer Battle," J.A. Blummer Manuscript, Research Files, CBNM.

Wooden Leg segment was Big Beaver, then about seventeen years of age. It was he who witnessed the shooting, and he later told Marquis. Yet, for some unexplained reason, Marquis has credited Wooden Leg with the observation. There are other things Big Beaver told Marquis, such as the death of a soldier which he witnessed, near the present east fence on Custer's battlefield. He told Marquis that two Cheyennes had done the killing. In *Wooden Leg*, Marquis describes this incident, but names as his informant *not* Big Beaver, but Wooden Leg, and then Marquis proceeds to change the homicide to a suicide, again for unexplained reasons. In light of these irregularities, one wonders about the credibility of the suicide theory, of which Marquis was an advocate.[33]

The battle around Custer Hill resulted in several more Indian casualties. One of these was the Cheyenne, Cut Belly, who probably was known among the Lakotas as the owner of a very pretty sorrel pony. Cut Belly sustained a gunshot wound while crossing the bench near the present cemetery, west of Custer Hill. He may have been removed from the field during the battle, possibly by three Cheyennes who were seen riding abreast, carrying a limp body.[34]

A number of casualties resulted from the combat activities on the west slope, below Custer Hill. The Cheyennes told Marquis that a Lakota was killed here, early in that part of the fight. In spite of this killing, young men continued to exhibit their prowess, among which was the Hunkpapa, Little Bear. Charging at the soldiers on the hill, his grey pinto was killed right under him, while he himself was disabled moments later from a gunshot to his leg. Fortunately, he was rescued by his friend, Elk Nation, who braved heavy firing to bring him back to safety.[35]

[33]Ibid.; Marquis, *Wooden Leg*, p. 233, Marquis, *Keep the Last Bullet for Yourself*.

[34]Marquis, *Wooden Leg*, p. 268; DeMallie, *The Sixth Grandfather*, p. 186.

[35]Marquis, *Keep the Last Bullet*, p. 158; DeMallie, *The Sixth Grandfather*, p. 191.

Shortly after Little Bear's rescue, military resistance on Custer Hill seemed to have collapsed, and soldiers were seen rushing down the slope, toward the Little Bighorn below. Among those who watched this movement was Iron Hawk, who had gathered with a large band of Hunkpapas on the flats near the mouth of Deep Ravine:

> We looked up and the soldiers all were running toward the Hunkpapas on foot. I had nothing but bow and arrows. Someone on the right side began charging first—his name was Red Horn Buffalo. The Hunkpapas said: "Hokahey!" and charged at them. The soldiers were running downhill and the Hunkpapas were charging. When they saw us, the soldiers swung down and Red Horn Buffalo rode right into the soldiers. This was the last we saw of this man. The Hunkpapas ran right up to the soldiers and encircled them from all sides. I noticed that Red Horn Buffalo's horse was going all alone, empty saddled.[36]

Red Horn Buffalo survived his injuries, because his name does not appear on the Hunkpapa dead roll. This brave Hunkpapa is not to be confused with an Oglala namesake. The Oglala, Red Horn Buffalo, sustained a gunshot in the jaw while pursuing Reno's troopers. He fell midstream, but miraculously he did not drown, and was unconscious when pulled from the river. He wore a rawhide brace on his jaw for many months while living on soup and water. This crude but effective medical device probably saved his life. He passed away at a ripe old age, at Pine Ridge in 1920.[37]

The escape of survivors from Custer Hill was witnessed by Big Beaver, who was then near the top, on the north side. His observations were recorded by Joe A. Blummer, of which an extract follows:

> ...He saw them all rushing up towards the hill to where the monument is. He stated that he went up also, and when he got up

---

[36]DeMallie, *The Sixth Grandfather*, p. 191.
[37]John P. Colhoff to Chas. D. Schreideis, April 30, 1943, Spring Collection.

there no soldiers were standing up, but some were still firing that
were on the ground, or sitting up. The Indians rushed them and
that was the end there, but he says some men, about fifteen, got
over to the west or on the E Troop position and ran for the river,
right down the coulee. Here, he says, these soldiers were scared as
they did not shoot back, and that the Indians ran them down. Now
these men were out of ammunition and could not shoot back. They
were trying to make it to the brush along the river. That is the way
he [Big Beaver] saw it. He says they just ran towards the river—
these men made a run towards the river to try to save themselves by
hiding in the brush on the river bank. My [J.A. Blummer's] idea is
that they used all their ammunition and were making the last effort
to get away.[38]

However, Lakotas insist that these soldiers had discarded
their carbines, and were armed with revolvers. They state
further that the soldiers were firing straight up into the air,
without taking any aim, and that in general they displayed
erratic behavior. Although Big Beaver estimated the soldiers
at fifteen, the Hunkpapa, Good Voiced Elk, had a clear view
of them further down the slope, and he told Walter Camp:

> Those who broke from the end of ridge and tried to get away by
> running toward the river, were dismounted. There was a deep gully
> without any water in it. I saw many jump over the steep bank into
> this gully in their effort to escape, but these were all killed. There
> were probably 25 or 30 of them.[39]

The Minneconjou, Standing Bear, confirms Good Voiced
Elk's observations. Standing Bear had worn a stuffed redbird
on his head as his spiritual protector, and he had made a
sacred vow so as to keep from being wounded. However, this
young boy withdrew from Custer Hill, mindful of the fact
that the Indians had shot some of their own men:

> After the soldiers went toward the Little Big Horn they went

---

[38]"Big Beaver's Story," Blummer Manuscript, CBNM.
[39]Walter Mason Camp Papers, Robert Spurrier Ellison Collection, Denver Public
Library, Item 6.

into the side of a hill, into a draw and there was tall grass in here. We were right on top of the soldiers and there was no use in their hiding from us. Then I saw an Indian rush at the men and the Indians killed every soldier, including some of our own Indians who had gone ahead of the rest.[40]

One of the landscape features most frequently visited on Custer's battlefield is a dry gully named Deep Ravine. Here, in 1876, the Military buried some twenty-eight of their own. Perhaps a brief description of this gully might benefit the reader. Deep Ravine extends north for about a mile from its junction with the Little Bighorn to the divide on Last Stand Hill. A tributary, named Calhoun Coulee, branches off at the lower fork and extends southeasterly to Calhoun Ridge. Some six hundred yards above its mouth, Deep Ravine curves to form a prominent bend. It was this bend which Captain McDougall pointed out to Walter Camp in 1909 as the location where he buried twenty-eight soldiers in 1876. This location also marks the approximate site where two Indian boys were fatally wounded, allegedly by their own people.[41]

Among the Indian casualties in Deep Ravine was a Cheyenne boy known to the Lakotas for his left-handed dexterity. They called him Left Hand, the son of Ice. Nonetheless, a hasty Sioux mistook him for an enemy scout and shot him on the bottom of Deep Ravine. This young victim is remembered among his own people as Noisy Walking, the son of White Bull, a respected Cheyenne.[42]

Referring to Noisy Walking, Willis Rowland learned that Thunder Walking had charged headlong into Custer's troopers at the height of the fight. It seems very likely, therefore, that Noisy Walking was disabled by a gunshot fired by a

[40]DeMallie, *The Sixth Grandfather*, p. 187.

[41]W.M. Camp to Gen. Godfrey, Nov. 6, 1920, Godfrey Family Papers, Army War College Library.

[42]White Bull Interview (1930); Camp Manuscript, IU, p. 91.

trooper. However, later examination of his wounds by his friend Wooden Leg revealed that he had been hit by as many as three bullets, only one of which had exited at the back. Moreover, the side of the chest showed several gashes, inflicted by repeated stabbings with a spear.[43]

There exists some confusion about the actual location where Noisy Walking was mortally wounded. John Stands in Timber told Peter Powell that this site was marked by boulders, and that its location was only 150 feet west of Lame White Man's kill site. This, of course, is an obvious error, and in sharp contrast with the historical statements. Wooden Leg made it very clear that Noisy Walking was wounded "down in the gulch where the band of soldiers nearest the river had been killed." This is corroborated by Noisy Walking's aunt, Big Head Woman, who recovered her nephew's body "in a deep gulch half way to the river," indicating the area of the big bend in Deep Ravine.[44]

After Noisy Walking was lashed to a pony travois, he was taken by his relatives to the Cheyenne camp across the river. He was visited after sundown by Wooden Leg, who left us a sad glimpse of his dying friend, Noisy Walking:

> He was lying on a ground bed of buffalo robes under a willow dome shelter. His father, White Bull, was with him. His mother sat just outside the entrance. I asked my friend: "How are you?" He replied: "Good, only I want water." I did not know what else to say but I wanted him to know that I was his friend and willing to do whatever I could for him. I sat down upon the ground beside him. After a little while I said: "You were very brave." Nothing else was said for several minutes. He was weak. His hands trembled at every move he made. Finally he said to his father: "I wish I could have some water—just a little of it." "No. Water will kill you." White Bull almost choked as he said this to his son. But he was a good

[43]*Billings Gazette*, May 26, 1927; Marquis, *Wooden Leg*, p. 241.
[44]Peter J. Powell, *Sweet Medicine*, Vol II, p. 119; Marquis, *Wooden Leg*, p. 241; Marquis, *Custer on the Little Bighorn*, p. 40.

medicine man, and he knew what was best. As I sat there looking at Noisy Walking, I knew he was going to die. My heart was heavy. But I could not do him any good, so I excused myself and went away.[45]

Noisy Walking died during the night of June 25. He was buried the following afternoon in a crevice along the rim-rocks, west of the Cheyenne camp. Remnants of his and other Cheyenne burials could be seen as late as 1916, after which date vandals desecrated the Indian remains.[46] In addition to Noisy Walking, at least one other Indian casualty was sustained in Deep Ravine. According to the Oglala, Fears Nothing, an Indian in pursuit of fleeing troopers had stumbled into a ravine, among the soldiers, and was killed by them. Although one could construe this to be a reference to Noisy Walking, I do not think so because Fears Nothing reported only on the casualties among the Lakotas.[47] Moreover, Wooden Leg confirmed the killing of two Lakotas near Noisy Walking, one of whom was an Oglala who was slain in the ravine.[48] This observation is corroborated by the Hunkpapa, Lone Man, and recorded by Walter Camp:

[Lone Man] says there was a Sioux Indian in deep gully with 28 soldiers. At first thought he was with the soldiers, but later found that he was a hostile who had followed the soldiers too closely. Even his own people had mutilated the body, thinking it was that of the Indian scouts with the soldiers.[49]

The identity of this slain Lakota is not known, nor do we know the name or tribal affiliation of the second Lakota casualty, mentioned by Wooden Leg. Perhaps the latter vic-

---

[45]Marquis, *Wooden Leg*, pp. 255-56.
[46]Marquis, *Custer on the Little Bighorn*, p. 40; Maine, *Lone Eagle…the White Sioux*, p. 132.
[47]Respects (Fears) Nothing Interview, Ricker Collection.
[48]Marquis, *Wooden Leg*, p. 243; Marquis, *Keep the Last Bullet*, p. 160.
[49]Camp Manuscript, IU, p. 350.

tim was the nephew of the Minneconjou, Turtle Rib, whose young relative was killed by a soldier's bullet at the end of the battle, near Custer Hill. That there were at least two dead Lakotas is confirmed by the Oglala, Black Elk. As a young boy, he saw the wailing relatives of these dead men wrap the two bodies in blankets, and carry the remains on pony travoises back to their camps.[50]

From his position on Custer Hill, Black Elk spotted yet another Lakota casualty on the west slope below, and he witnessed the compassionate grief which followed:

> I saw some men holding up a man and when we went over there I found it was Chase in the Morning's brother called Black Wasichu. A few feet from here there were several soldiers wounded. Black Wasichu was still living and they were giving him some medicine. He was shot through the right shoulder, downward, and the ball lodged in the left hip, because he was leaning on the side of his horse when he was shot. My father and Black Wasichu's father got so mad about the latter's son getting wounded that they went and butchered a white man and cut him open.[51]

The injury to Black Wasichu proved to be fatal, and he passed away during the night of June 27. His body was sepulchered on a scaffold along Wood Louse Creek, at the foot of the Big Horn Mountains. His full name was *Wasicun Sapa,* with the English translation being Black White Man, possibly denoting a captive of African descent.[52]

At least one Indian casualty occurred near the mouth of Deep Ravine, probably near the end of the Custer battle. Many years later, the Minneconjou, Feather Earring, told of this dead Lakota, and the fate of his killer.

> I drove five horses across the river, gray horses, they were all wounded and trembling. I saw they were mortally wounded and let

[50]Hammer, *Custer in '76*, p. 201; DeMallie, *The Sixth Grandfather*, p. 194.
[51]DeMallie, *The Sixth Grandfather*, p. 194.
[52]Ibid., p. 198.

them go and went back toward monument ridge. About 200 yards
from the river, I saw two bodies and went to look at them. One was
a dead Indian, the other a white man alongside him. I saw the white
man's heart beating and called to a Sioux, "Your grandfather has
been killed by the man alongside of him; I don't think he is dead;
you had better shoot him." He came up and put an arrow through
him; he [the soldier] jumped up and was shot and killed by another
arrow; he had been playing dead.[53]

The name and tribal affiliation of this Lakota is not
known. He probably was an elderly man, because Feather
Earring spoke of him by using the respectful term of "grand-
father." Although speculation, the white man near this dead
Lakota may have been Trumpeter Henry C. Dose, who was
assigned to Headquarters' Staff as Custer's personal orderly.
Dose was found a short distance above the lower fork of
Deep Ravine, with arrows shot in his back and sides.[54]

There is one more Indian casualty which deserves our
attention. After the Custer Fight had ended, many women
and children ascended the battlefield to remove their relatives, the dead and the wounded. They vented their grief on
the disabled soldiers, and then pillaged the bodies. One of
those who saw the field was Cannonball Woman, who was
later known among the whites as Hattie Lawrence. As a ten-
year-old Hunkpapa girl, she stared with fright at many dead
soldiers in a gully, some of whom were lying on top of each
other. Being of very impressionable age, she had noted that
the bodies had turned black, and that amidst this scene of
horror an Indian was lying dead.[55]

The reference to black bodies suggests to me that the
remains were in an advanced state of decomposition. It follows logically, therefore, that this Hunkpapa girl did not

[53]Graham, *The Custer Myth*, pp. 97-98.
[54]Hardorff, *The Custer Burials*, pp. 111-12.
[55]Camp Manuscripts, IU, p. 347.

make her observation on the day of the battle, June 25, but rather on the day thereafter. If that was the case, one wonders why the body of this slain Indian was not removed. One explanation would be that the victim was a young man from the agencies, who did not have any close relations among the northern Indians. Or, perhaps, in all the confusion, his absence was not noticed immediately, or it did not cause any alarm as yet.

Eventually, the continued absence of this individual must have caused grave concern among his relations. It stands to reason, therefore, that they earnestly sought to learn his whereabouts. According to the Hunkpapa, Two Bulls, a woman was seen searching on Custer's battlefield, while the moon was rising full above. In view of the old-time Indian aversion for the dead during the night, such an act was incomprehensible, and in my mind could only mean one thing: This bereaved woman had disregarded all her super-stitions, to look for the body of a loved one among all these terrible ghostly sights.[56]

We will never know if she found the object of her search. However, two days after the battle, a military survivor spot-ted a dark body among the slain in Deep Ravine. Without making the actual identification, he thought he recognized the remains of Michel Bouyer, a Crow interpreter with the Army, whose mother was a Santee Indian.[57]

While standing on Calhoun Ridge ten years after the bat-tle, the Hunkpapa, Gall, pointed out to a gathering the loca-tions where Indians had died. According to Gall, eleven had been killed in the vicinity of Calhoun Ridge, "four over there," probably meaning Custer Hill, and "two in that coulee," indicating Deep Ravine. Of particular interest is the fact that Gall's total of seventeen casualties tallies closely

---

[56] Two Bulls Interview, Campbell Collection, Box 105, Notebook 35.
[57] Hammer, *Custer in '76*, p. 95.

with a roster of sixteen names now known to be the Indian dead of Custer's battle.[58]

Fatality	Location
Bear with Horns, Hunkpapa	along Custer Ridge
Guts, Hunkpapa	location unknown
Red Face, Hunkpapa	location unknown
Cloud Man, Sans Arc	location unknown
Lone Dog, Sans Arc	location unknown
Elk Bear, Sans Arc	location unknown
Kills Him, Sans Arc	location unknown
Bad Light Hair, Oglala	location unknown
Black White Man, Oglala	west slope Custer Hill (wounded)
Many Lice, Oglala	location unknown
Young Skunk, Oglala	location unknown
Black Bear, Cheyenne	north slope Custer Hill
Lame White Man, Cheyenne	halfway down Custer Ridge
Limber Bones, Cheyenne	north slope Custer Hill
Noisy Walking, Cheyenne	big bend Deep Ravine (wounded)
Open Belly, Cheyenne	near present museum (wounded)

---

[58] *St. Paul Pioneer Press*, July 15, 1886.

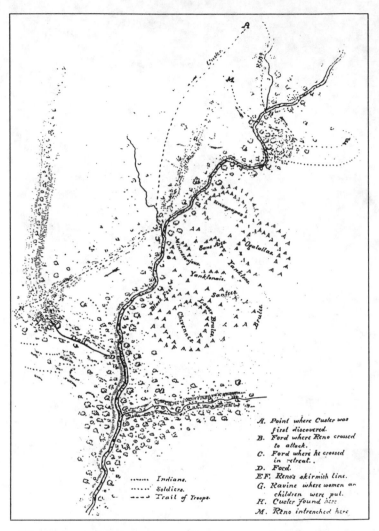

A. *Point where Custer was first discovered.*
B. *Ford where Reno crossed to attack.*
C. *Ford where he crossed in retreat.*
D. *Ford.*
E F. *Reno's skirmish line.*
G. *Ravine where women and children were put.*
H. *Custer found here.*
M. *Reno intrenched here.*

······ Indians.
······ Soldiers.
- - - - Trail of Troops.

This worn and faded map was found among the Elizabeth B. Custer Collection at Custer Battlefield National Monument. It was made by Capt. John S. Poland, 6th Infantry, from tracings made for him by an Indian who claimed to have taken part in the fight. Poland drew it within a few weeks of the battle while he was stationed at Standing Rock Indian Reservation. *Courtesy Custer Battlefield National Monument.*

CHAPTER FOUR

The Reno Hill Fight

Of the three phases of the Little Bighorn fight, the one dealing with the defense of Reno Hill is probably the best documented. Through the many eyewitness statements and modern science, we have been able to determine the precise theatre of action, the locations where heavy combat took place, and the sites where military casualties were sustained.

Before focussing on the Indian casualties, it might be beneficial to give a brief outline of the Reno Hill fight. After being routed to the bluffs across the river, Major Marcus A. Reno's disorganized battalion was soon joined by that of Captain Frederick W. Benteen coming up from the rear. A short time after this junction, one company advanced north, to where the sound of Custer's firing was heard. This advance was followed later by the balance of the regiment after the packtrain had arrived.

The farthest point reached on this advance was a cluster of knobs identified as Weir Point, which elevations allowed an unobstructed view of Custer's battlefield. Nothing was seen, however, of Custer's troops, and soon hordes of Indians were seen converging towards Weir Point. Finding this location unsuitable for defense, orders were given to fall back to Reno Hill. Here, the balance of the regiment gallantly resisted a superior Indian force for two days, before being relieved by a supporting military column.[1]

During the fight for Reno Hill, the Indians sustained a number of casualties. One of these was the Hunkpapa, Powder Side, who was shot just north of the entrenchments, by K Company troopers who covered Reno's retreat. Powder Side's gunshot wound was not a fatal injury, since his name is not listed among the Lakota dead. But others were not so fortunate. One of these was a young Lakota boy who was slain on June 25, near dusk. According to the Minneconjou, Standing Bear, this Indian rider had been charging close to the soldiers. However, his show of bravery had abruptly ended when he was shot on the east side of Reno Hill.[2]

The location where this boy lay was exposed to the gunfire by the soldiers, and as a result, it was not until nightfall that his body was removed. According to the Hunkpapa, Old Bull, the name of this young Lakota was Breech Cloth, but his Lakota tribal affiliation seems to have been forgotten.[3] Many years later, the Cheyenne, Stands in Timber, learned from the Sioux the meaning of a small pile of rocks, east of Reno Hill:

> On Reno field, some rocks east of the soldier position mark where a 15-year-old Sioux boy rode too close to the soldiers and was killed. His horse threw him, then the boy was shot. The horse turned over in the air and then got up and ran away.[4]

Although Breech Cloth was killed on June 25, the other

---

[1]Although much new evidence has come to light since its publication, Stewart's *Custer's Luck*, pp. 408-30, presents, perhaps, the finest reconstruction of the Reno Hill fight, from an Army viewpoint.

[2]DeMallie, *The Sixth Grandfather*, pp. 187, 192.

[3]Ibid., p. 187; Old Bull Interview, Campbell Collection, Box 105, Notebook 11.

[4]John Stands in Timber Interview, CBNM.

Indian fatalities occurred on the second day of fighting, June 26, when the Indians renewed their attack with vigor. The firing began at daybreak, about two a.m. local time, and went on relentlessly until about nine a.m., when it subsided to desultory firing by noon. During this period two Lakotas lost their lives.

Around 8:30 a.m. local time, the Indians made a desperate attempt to charge Reno Hill from the south side. In this attack they nearly succeeded in reaching the soldiers' breastworks. According to General Edward S. Godfrey's narrative account:

> An Indian had shot one of [Lt. Francis M.] Gibson's men, and then rushed up and touched the body with his "coup-stick," and started back to cover, but he was killed. He was in such close proximity to the lines and so exposed to the fire that the other Indians could not carry his body away. This, I believe, was the only dead Indian left in our possession; that is, at Reno Hill. This boldness determined Benteen to make a charge, and the Indians were driven nearly to the river.[5]

However, one of the troopers who partook in this charge recalled this matter somewhat differently:

> In Benteen's charge, the Indians had formed in the gully and were coming up the hill. We charged out, Old Benteen right in front of us. Before this charge the Indians had been close enough to throw stones in our lines. When we charged out we killed three of them. The Indian who was killed and whom the Indians could not get was killed on the evening of June 25.[6]

It should be noted that the Indian sources do not corroborate the claim of Indian fatalities sustained during the soldiers' counter attack. Moreover, the Indian killed near the south side of the breastworks was positively slain on June 26.

---

[5] Graham, *The Custer Myth*, pp. 144-45.
[6] Hammer, *Custer in '76*, p. 105.

Furthermore, there seems to exist some confusion as to when and how this Lakota boy was killed.[7]

According to Godfrey's account, the boy was killed after counting coup on a dead soldier and while running back to his own lines. This is also the official version, published in the guidebooks at Custer Battlefield. It differs, however, by stating that the boy was shot *after* Benteen had made his counter charge.[8]

Careful examination of the evidence provided by other military sources presents a different picture of this minor incident. According to Lieutenant Francis M. Gibson, who was on Benteen's line, the Lakota had been killed *before* Benteen's charge took place. This statement is confirmed by Captain Myles Moylan, who added that this Indian had come to within fifteen or twenty yards of the line when he was shot. Other witnesses stated that this Lakota had a belt full of ammunition slung over his shoulder, a sheath knife clamped between his teeth, and a revolver in each hand, leading other Indians on a charge.[9]

The killing of this Lakota was described by Private Edward Pigford to Walter M. Camp, who wrote it down as follows:

> [Pigford] says Indian killed near H Co line was one who had charged up and stopped there. The soldiers had fled to north end of Benteen's line. Every so often this Indian would rise and fire. Once when he rose up he exposed the upper half of his body, and Pigford, taking deliberate aim, killed him.[10]

According to the Minneconjou, One Bull, this young

[7]Major Reno's "Official Report," in Utley, *The Reno Court of Inquiry*, p. 385; Hammer, *Custer in '76*, p. 81.

[8](Don Ricky), *Entrenchment Trail*, p. 14.

[9]Hammer, *Custer in '76*, p. 81; Utley, *The Reno Court of Inquiry*, p. 212; Camp Manuscripts, IU, p. 678; Walter Camp Notes, BYU, p. 173.

[10]Hammer, *Custer in '76*, p. 144.

Lakota victim was known among his own people, the Sans Arcs, as *Canku Hanska,* or Long Road. This is confirmed by One Bull's brother, White Bull, who told Walter Campbell of the killing. We know that White Bull had a hearing impairment, but it appears that Campbell's stenographer had troubles also, because he recorded the name of the Sans Arc as Long *Robe,* instead of Long *Road.* It seems quite possible that Long Road had a nickname, because the Minneconjou, Flying By, identified him as Eagle Hat, and confirmed the latter's tribal affiliation with the Sans Arcs.[11]

The location of Long Road's kill site may be determined with a degree of reasonable accuracy. On the night of June 26, Lieutenant Charles A. Varnum had gone to Benteen's vacated entrenchments to greet the arrival of several men presumed missing in action. Varnum had gone up Benteen's bluff and had barely stepped off the bench when he stumbled over the remains of a dead Indian.[12] In a letter to Earl A. Brininstool, Lieutenant Varnum discloses additional details pertaining to this matter:

> You know, of course, that on evening of June 26th, we moved our position to some extent. The up-stream flank of our position became the down-stream flank, and we extended it toward the river and fortified it some... I had just got well fixed for a nap when I heard a picket challenge and DeRudio answered: "It is me—Lieut. DeRudio and Sergt. O'Neill." I was some distance down from the bluff when I heard the challenge and answer. I ran up the slope, calling to DeRudio to wait till I got there, as he would fall into gullies if he tried to come to my voice where I was. As I arrived at the crest near the gully, I stumbled over something and fell over a dead Indian... In 1898, on Decoration Day, I visited the field with a party from Sheridan, Wyoming, where I was buying horses... I was standing where I thought I found that Indian's body and spoke of it, and how I happened to be there, etc., when a newspaper man

---

[11]Camp Manuscripts, IU, pp. 349-50; White Bull interview (1932).
[12]Hammer, *Custer in '76,* p. 62.

said, "What is this?" Small round stones had been laid in a square
about two feet each way, and then built up with other small stones,
forming a sort of pyramid about four inches high. Sticks stuck in
the ground with red cloth bundles, medicine bags tied to them and
some other ornaments were there, and I said at once, "That is that
Indian's monument." This Indian was scalped by interpreter Fred
Girard [sic], and the scalp was given to a newspaper man in
Chicago when we were there at the Reno investigating board, or
Court of Inquiry; at least, Girard told me so when we were in
Chicago at that time.[13]

The location and stone marking of Long Road's kill site is
corroborated by the Cheyenne, Stands in Timber, who
learned that the Lakota boy was known among the
Cheyennes by the name of Thunder Shield. He gained this
information from his fellow tribesman, Little Shield, and an
Oglala named White Dress, from Pine Ridge. Stands in
Timber was told that Long Road had followed an older
Lakota during the charge and was killed near the soldier line.
It was said that Long Road had lost an older brother a week
earlier during the battle of the Rosebud. The grieving relatives saw he had grown despondent by his brother's death,
and they knew that he did not want to live anymore.[14]

According to Stands in Timber, two large rocks, one on
each side of a small draw, still mark the place where Long
Road was killed. A very short distance north of here is the
site where Private Thomas E. Meador of H Company was
slain. The proximity between the two kill sites is affirmed by
the Minneconjou, One Bull, who stated that Long Road
died about seventy five feet from the soldiers' line.[15]

Long Road was slain inside the present iron fence on Reno
Hill, where a small pile of rocks still marks his kill site. Out-

[13]E.A. Brininstool, *Troopers with Custer*, pp. 150-51.
[14]John Stands in Timber Interview, CBNM; Stands in Timber and Liberty, *Cheyenne Memories*, p. 207.
[15]Stands in Timber and Liberty, *Cheyenne Memories*, p. 207; Camp Manuscripts, IU, p. 350.

side the fence, in line with the soldiers' position on the hill and Long Road's kill site lower down, nine bullets were found, the intervals marking the progress of Long Road's charge and the courage of his conviction.[16]

The second Lakota fatality on Reno Hill was the Minneconjou, Dog's Back Bone, whose son, Kingman, was an allottee at Cheyenne River Indian Agency as late as 1930. According to the Hunkpapa, Old Bull, Dog's Back Bone was killed while yelling a warning to his tribesmen to exercise caution—"Be careful[!] It's a long way from here but their bullets are coming fierce." As Dog's Back Bone finished his warning, he was shot in the head and was instantly killed. The death of this Lakota is confirmed by his brother, Takes the Horses, and another Minneconjou, Flying By, the son of Lame Deer.[17]

There exists some confusion about the date of Dog's Back Bone's killing and the location where it took place. According to the Minneconjou, White Bull, Dog's Back Bone was shot in the head and killed near him, northeast of Reno Hill, on June 25. However, the Hunkpapa, Old Bull, maintains that the killing took place the day after Custer was killed, June 26, during the middle of the day. He identified the location as being northeast of Reno Hill, about a quarter of a mile east of the river.[18]

Old Bull remembered the details very clearly because the battle had started early that morning, June 26, but he had been unable to join until midday when the fighting subsided. Old Bull's recollection is corroborated by the Minneconjou, Standing Bear, who recalled the incident as having taken

[16]Henry and Don Weibert, *Sixty-six Years in Custer's Shadow*, p. 105.

[17]Old Bull Interview, Campbell Collection, Box 105, Notebook 11; White Bull Interview (1932); Camp Manuscripts, IU, pp. 238, 349.

[18]White Bull Interviews (1930, and 1932); Old Bull Interview, Campbell Collection, Box 105, Notebook 11.

Flanked by their interpreters, these twelve Lakota veterans of the Custer Fight were photographed by Earl E. Brininstool at Custer Battlefield, 1926. Standing, left to right: Jim Red Cloud, Red Hawk, Eagle Bear, Makes Enemy, Standing Bear, Sitting Hawk, White Bull, and Charles Little Hawk; sitting, left to right: Blind Water, Eagle Chase, Black Elk, Little Warrior, Little Horse, and Frank Conroy. *Courtesy Custer Battlefield National Monument.*

place on June 26. He remembered the particulars from looking at the dead body of his tribesman, especially the gaping
bullet hole above the eyebrow in the victim's forehead.[19]

In addition to the recollections of the Indian informants,
we have a number of military eyewitnesses whose testimony
suggests additional Indian casualties. Among the latter was
Private Edward Pigford of M Company, who made the following revelation to Walter M. Camp:

> While men were getting water on pm on June 26, he with others
> was guarding the route and saw an Indian in a tree on west side of
> river. He put up his sights and fired at him and saw him fall. On
> June 27, they found this Indian with a wound in his thigh and his
> neck broken. He had fallen out of the tree when shot and appar-
> ently had landed on his head and had died there. Apparently, none
> of the Indians had found him.[20]

Although this statement by itself appears to have a ring of
truth, it loses considerable credibility from a later Pigford
story. Gifted with a vivid imagination, Private Pigford
claimed that this very same Indian had been firing arrows at
him from a *shotgun!*[21]

In addition to Pigford's doubtful claim, we also know that
Captain Thomas H. French had cut a notch in the stock of
his rifle for killing an Indian on June 26. In addition, Captain
Thomas M. McDougall recalled a particular incident on the
same day, when a brave Indian taunted the troopers for a very
long time. This Indian was dressed in the clothing of a slain

[19]Old Bull Interview; DeMallie, *The Sixth Grandfather*, p. 189.
[20]Hammer, *Custer in '76*, p. 144.
[21]Carroll, *The Benteen-Goldin Letters*, p. 100.

trooper, and he was galloping back and forth, parading a captured company guidon. At last, he was hit by a gunshot fired
by the enraged troopers, and he was seen falling from his
pony. Captain Frederick W. Benteen also claimed to have
shot an Indian early on June 26. However, since all these
claims lack confirmation, it may well be that all these casualties sustained non-fatal injuries.[22]

One of the more puzzling matters involving Indian casualties is an observation made by Private John Burkman after
the Reno Hill fight. In order to do justice to Burkman's recollection, it is, perhaps, best to explain this matter first through
the words of Sergeant John M. Ryan:

> Late in the day [of June 26] the fire of the Indians slackened,
> except on the point of a high bluff in the direction of which it was
> supposed that Custer had gone. Here the Indians put in a few well-
> directed shots that laid several of our men low. I do not know what
> kind of gun one of those Indians used, but it made a tremendous
> noise, and, in fact, those Indians were out of range of our carbine,
> which were Springfields, caliber .45. Capt. French of my company
> asked me if I could do anything with those Indians, as they were
> out of range of the carbines. I told the Captain that I would try, and
> as I was the owner of a 15-pound Sharp's telescope rifle, caliber .45,
> which I had made in Bismarck before the expedition started out,
> and which cost me $100. I fired a couple of shots until I got range of
> that group of Indians. Then I put in half a dozen shots in rapid suc-
> cession, and those Indians scampered away from that point of the
> bluff, and that ended the firing on the part of the Indians in that
> memorable engagement, and the boys set up quite a cheer.[23]

John Burkman witnessed this same incident and related
additional details to his biographer, I.D. O'Donnell, who
recorded it in the vernacular of the grizzled trooper:

> All durin' the twenty-fifth and sixth whilst the Indians down
> below was firin' up at us they was a fellow on a hill overlookin' ours

[22]Graham, *The Custer Myth*, pp. 244, 341; Hammer, *Custer in '76*, p. 71.
[23]Graham, *The Custer Myth*, p. 245.

that kept poppin' down at us with a long range buffalo gun. He was a good shot. We couldn't see him but every time his gun popped, down dropped one o' our men or a horse or a mule. That Indian did more to pester us than all the bunch down below. Toward the last Captain Ryan got him with a long range gun. After the fight I went over the hill and seen him layin' thar, the buffalo gun still in his hand, back o' some boulders he'd piled up for breastworks.[24]

On June 28, Reno's force left Reno Hill and travelled north along the bluffs to Custer's battlefield. However, since Burkman did not accompany the regiment, we do not know when he made this observation. No other source mentions the discovery of an Indian body on the elevation north of Reno Hill, and considering the zeal with which the Indians recovered their dead, the abandonment of a slain tribesman appears very unlikely. Indeed, General Godfrey would later write that the only dead Indian found on the bluffs was the young boy slain near Benteen's line. Yet, I find it difficult to dismiss that which Burkman claims he saw with his own eyes.[25]

There is one more matter which needs to be addressed. It was rumored among the survivors that white men collaborated with the Indians and had fought against the troopers pinned on Reno Hill. Many years after these events, Frank Huston, an ex-confederate, revealed that there were white men in the Indian camps—not among the Sioux, but among the other nations present. Huston had an intense hatred for the Yankees, stemming from the brutal murder of his mother by drunken Union soldiers. Rather than surrendering in 1865, he preferred an allegiance with the Sioux with whom he lived until 1881. Some are convinced, therefore, that Huston himself had fought against the Blue at the Little Bighorn.[26]

---

[24]Glendolin D. Wagner, *Old Neutriment*, pp. 169-70.
[25]Ibid., p. 182; Graham, *The Custer Myth*, p. 145.

The Indians themselves have shown a reluctance to confirm the presence of white collaborators. One notable exception was the Oglala, He Dog, who guardedly acknowledged the allegation and admitted that there was a white man in the Oglala camp. He Dog rationalized the white man's presence by identifying him as a Canadian half-breed, who spoke very good English, and Lakota as well.[27] Perhaps the most compromising evidence was provided by Sergeant M.H. Wilson of the Seventh U.S. Infantry, who marched with Gibbon's Montana Column to the Little Bighorn. From an interview with Wilson, Walter M. Camp recorded:

> On June 26, Gibbon's march was on west side of Little Bighorn all the way from the buttes east of Big Horn. Crossed Little Bighorn to its west side at these buttes about 6 miles above its mouth and then kept on west all the way up. At the bend ([of present] Crow Agency) next morning kept over to foothills and on same side of river. At the first coulee, there were three or four big cottonwoods (about west of Curley's [present] ranch) and found a white man with long beard buried in a tree. Wilson helped take him down. He was dressed as an Indian and was evidently fighting with them and killed on Reno Hill where he had been seen by soldiers. Was shot in five or six places.[28]

Since the remains were discovered on June 26, the question remains whether this individual could have been a casualty of the Custer battle of the preceding day. Moreover, it seems difficult to explain why the body was sepulchered some ten miles north of Custer's battlefield, from which direction the Indians knew troop reinforcements were coming. Who this white man was, and why he was buried where he was found, will probably forever remain unanswered.[29]

---

[26]Reno's "Official Report," in Utley, *Reno Court of Inquiry*, p. 385; Graham, *The Custer Myth*, pp. 79-80.

[27]Hammer, *Custer in '76*, p. 206.

[28]Walter Camp Manuscripts, IU, pp. 72-73.

[29]See also the *New York Herald*, Aug. 1, 1876, which makes reference to white collaborators, among which was a bearded man.

The following list reflects the names of Lakotas slain on Reno Hill.

Fatality	Location
Breech Cloth, Lakota tribe unknown	east side Reno Hill, 6/25
Long Road, Sans Arc	south side Reno Hill, 6/26
Dog's Back Bone, Minneconjou	northeast of Reno Hill, 6/26

Contrasted starkly against the grey sky, this photo of an old lantern slide of unknown origin and date shows the Lakota way of scaffold and lodge burials. These methods, in addition to tree burials, were used at the Little Bighorn in 1876. *Courtesy Custer Battlefield National Monument.*

CHAPTER FIVE

A Stillness after the Battle

With the arrival of the Montana Column on Tuesday, June 27, a number of the officers recorded their impressions about the Indian dead left behind in the valley. These observations are essential to our study, since they provide us with a means to test the accuracy of the totals obtained from Indian sources. One of the officers who kept a diary was Captain Walter Clifford of the Seventh U.S. Infantry:

> June 27—Resumed the march at 7 a.m. Quite a number of Indian ponies were picked up, and upon reaching a low hill, could plainly see two skin lodges and a number of horses among the bottom timber. Capt. [Edward] Ball, 2nd Cavalry, had gone ahead and could be seen charging on a run, but at what we could not determine.
>
> Nearing the two lodges, we found the ground strewn with Indian camp equipage, bundles of lodge poles tied together, ready for moving, buffalo robes, saddles, cooking utensils, coffee-mills, china dishes—new ones—axes, guns, pistols, horn spoons, wooden soup bowls, all lying in the utmost confusion, as though this was the prelude to a hurried stampede. Numbers of Indian dogs were about. They fled like wolves at our approach. Everyone was possessed with a burning curiosity to examine the numerous articles lying scattered about, and often was the caution to the men to

"remain in the ranks" repeated. Double-barreled shotguns, rifles, knives and pistols of unique patterns were picked up by the men, only to be thrown away after being carried a short distance. In spite of the order of "silence, men," a low and continuous hum of voices could be heard.

Arriving at the lodges, we found a number of dead horses lying around them in a circle, shot. Inside the lodges were the bodies of eight warriors, lying in state—five in one lodge, three in the other.[1]

Other officers with the Montana Column confirm Captain Clifford's observation. Lieutenant Edward J. McClernand, Second U.S. Cavalry, also remembered seeing two lodges. The same number is reported by Lieutenant Edward Maguire, Corps of Engineers, who included this information in his *Annual Report* for 1876, and repeated it in 1877. Lieutenant Holmes O. Paulding, Assistant Surgeon, wrote of seeing two lodges also. And, finally, we have the statement by Colonel John Gibbon, Seventh U.S. Infantry, whose official report referred to "a large deserted Indian camp, in which two teepies [sic] were still standing."[2]

Unfortunately, relatively simple matters tend to turn into controversial subjects as a result of conflicting information. This is the case with the reported number of funeral lodges, and the count of bodies seen therein; the locations where these lodges stood; and the number of sites where other bodies had been sepulchered. Take, for example, Lieutenant Charles F. Roe, Second Cavalry, who observed the same scene described by Captain Clifford, but who gained a different impression nonetheless:

---

[1]Usher L. Burdick, *Tales from Buffalo Land: The Story of Fort Bufort*, pp. 51-52.

[2]Edward J. McClernand, *With the Indian and the Buffalo in Montana, 1870-1878*, p. 59; *Annual Report* of Lt. Edward Maguire, Year Ending June 30, 1876, Appendix 00 of the *Report of the Secretary of War*, Vol. II, Pt. III, p. 702; William Boyes, *Surgeon's Diary*, p. 23; Lloyd J. Overfield II, *The Little Big Horn, 1876: The Official Communications, Documents and Reports*, p. 84.

As I came around [the bend], being the rear guard, I saw the advance troop moving in the direction of three teepees or lodges, shining white in the morning sun. Arriving there, we found that they were funeral teepees, in one of which were five dead Indians and in the other three; around the outside were dead ponies, indicating that the slain warriors were chiefs. These teepees were hung with black blankets, the bodies raised a foot from the ground, with all their war bonnets, heavily beaded shirts, leggings and moccasins on them.[3]

Lieutenant Roe makes it clear that there were three lodges, but then he leaves us with the impression that only two contained dead bodies. However, Lieutenant Richard E. Thompson, Sixth U.S. Infantry, went so far as to check its contents. Many years later he told Walter M. Camp that these lodges contained respectively three, eight, and eleven bodies, all finely dressed.[4]

The possibility exists that Lieutenant Thompson's memory may have been playing mathematical tricks. His number "eight" may have been the sum of "five" and "three," which are the numbers reported by others who saw only two lodges. Ergo, Lieutenant Thompson's number "eleven" is the sum of his "eight" and "three." For that reason, I speculate that he may have seen the body totals of three, five and eight, instead. The sum of these numbers add up to sixteen, which is the exact body total spoken of by Lieutenant Paulding in a letter to his mother.[5]

Of the surviving Seventh Cavalry men, only a handful made reference to the funeral lodges. Perhaps this was due to the fact that they were occupied in bringing down the wounded from the bluff, after which they began the grim

[3]Charles F. Roe, "Custer's Last Battle," p. 10, in *Custer Engages the Hostiles.*
[4]Hammer, *Custer in '76*, p. 248.
[5]Thomas S. Buecker, "A Surgeon on the Little Big Horn," *Montana the Magazine of Western History* (Autumn, 1982):43.

task of burying their dead comrades. One who made mention of these lodges was Major Marcus A. Reno, who later wrote that the valley was strewn with Indian ponies, some still struggling in the agony of death, and that two teepees of fine white skin were left standing.[6]

Trumpeter John Martin also remembered seeing the two teepees, as did Lieutenant Winfield S. Edgerly, who added that one lodge contained five and the other six bodies, all "finely dressed and ornamented, and tied standing up to a vertical pole in each case." As much as I would like to believe Edgerly's observation, his statement about upright burials warrants definite skepticism since it is contrary to the Lakota way.[7]

The Cheyennes, however, have been known to occasionally bury their combat fatalities in a sitting position, the legs folded at the knees, with the feet turned to the right—much like the women's way of sitting. As a rule, however, the Cheyennes buried their dead by placing the remains in a fetal position, as if asleep, the body lying on its right side. In regards to Lieutenant Edgerly's observation, we know that the bodies in the funeral lodges were dead Sioux.[8]

For the benefit of the reader, an explanation of the Lakota way of burial might be in order. Lakota funerals were conducted according to a rigid ritual. After washing the dead man's body, relatives dressed the deceased in his burial clothes, consisting of a profusely beaded shirt and a pair of leggings, and moccasins with beaded soles. His face was painted red, over which colored symbols were applied to represent achievements. His hair was then combed and greased, after which feathers and other hair adornments were attached to the head.[9]

---

[6]Major Marcus A. Reno, "The Custer Massacre," copy in Custer Battlefield Study Collection, Roll 8.

[7]Hammer, *Custer in '76*, pp. 58, 105.

[8]Two Moons Interview, Campbell Collection, Box 105, Notebook 15.

To provide the dead man with symbolic subsistence to travel the Spirit Trail, a piece of buffalo suet was placed in the dead man's mouth. The body was then wrapped in a buffalo robe, along with his tools of war and other cherished possessions. This bundle was wrapped once more, using a tanned skin, the whole being securely tied with rawhide thongs. The sepulchered remains were now ready to be fastened to a scaffold. This elevated platform consisted of four forked posts, across which a frame was placed, the top raised high enough to discourage scavenger animals.[10]

Despite Lieutenant Edgerly's statement, we have sufficient evidence which suggests that the Sioux dead were sepulchered in the traditional Lakota way. One source is in the form of a letter, written by Sergeant Daniel A. Kanipe to his parents, immediately after the battle:

> We found three teepees with 75 Indians in them. I cut one of them out of the blankets and buffalo robes that he was wrapped in. When I did I found he had a string of scalps as long as your arm and among these were four women's, with hair as long as my arm, two of them having red hair, It was a sight![11]

Although Sergeant Kanipe unintentionally overestimated the body count, the fact remains that he had seen three teepees in which the dead had been sepulchered in buffalo robes. He repeated this statement twice later in life, but adjusted the estimate of the dead downward to sixty.[12]

To complicate matters more, there exists a diary which disputes the reported total of three lodges, suggesting that there were even more. Under the date of June 27, Captain Henry B. Freeman, Seventh U.S. Infantry, recorded that he

---

[9]Royal B. Hassrick, *The Sioux*, p. 335.

[10]Ibid., p. 336.

[11]Graham, *The Custer Myth*, p. 250.

[12]Daniel C. Kanipe, "A New Story of Custer's Last Battle," *Contributions to the Historical Society of Montana*, Vol. IV (1903), p. 282; Hammer, *Custer in '76*, p. 96.

"saw half a dozen lodges with dead Indians." Captain Freeman was a reliable witness whose diary cannot be ignored. The accuracy of his statement is born out by a similar observation by one of the Ree Indian Scouts who fought alongside the soldiers on Reno Hill. On June 26, Young Hawk saw the Sioux vacate their campsites, and he noticed that they left five lodges standing.[13]

A question arises about the possible locations of these five teepees. Since Young Hawk made his observation from Reno Hill, his vision down the river was limited due to protruding bluffs downstream, allowing him to see only the village site occupied on the morning of June 25. It should be noted further that on the same afternoon, the Indians moved their lodges farther downstream because of the Indian dead brought among them. In view of these facts, it seems likely, therefore, that the five lodges seen by Young Hawk, stood on the old village site of June 25.[14]

This conclusion appears to receive support from Young Hawk himself who examined the village site on June 27. He was then a member of Captain Benteen's detail entrusted with the preliminary identification of the officers slain on Custer's battlefield. After completing this difficult task, this detail crossed to the west side of the river at the mouth of Deep Ravine. Since they then travelled upstream—toward the site of Reno's valley fight—it appears that either Young Hawk, or his interviewer, was confused about the location he stated Bloody Knife was found.[15] Or else, although unlikely, the following observations were made by Young Hawk while going downstream:

[13]Henry B. Freeman Diary, copy in Edward S. Godfrey Family Papers, Army War College, Carlisle Barracks; Libby, *Arikara Narrative*, p. 106.

[14]Marquis, *Wooden Leg*, pp. 252-53.

[15]Hardorff, *Custer Battle Casualties*, pp. 17-18; Hammer, *Custer in '76*, pp. 86, 122.

They crossed lower down than where they had first crossed, a good watering place, right below Custer's hill. The body of Bloody Knife lay a little back from the brush near the ford. He saw evidence of fighting from the Custer hill clear to the river by the dead horses, though he saw no bodies of soldiers. The five teepees in the deserted Dakota camp were thrown down and some of the bodies stripped by the soldiers they had seen there. They went on to the Dakota camp and found the body of a dead Lakota lying on a tanned buffalo hide. Young Hawk recognized this warrior as one who had been a scout at Fort Lincoln, Chatka. He had on a white shirt, the shoulders were painted green, and on his forehead, painted in red, was the sign of a secret society. In the middle of the camp they found a drum and on one side, lying on a blanket, was a row of dead Dakotas with their feet toward the drum. Young Hawk supposed that a tent had covered them, with the entrance to the tent at the opposite where the dead bodies lay, that is, at the holy or back side of the tent. When alive, these braves would sit on the other side and drum. This drum was cut up and slashed. Farther on they found three more groups of dead Dakotas lying on canvas, buffalo hides, or blankets at the back side of where the tent had stood, that is, opposite the opening. All the fine buckskin shirts they had worn as well as beads and earrings had been stripped off by the soldiers. These groups of bodies were two, three, or four. In this camp they found evidence of great haste, bedding thrown away, bundles of dried meat dropped, etc.[16]

For the benefit of this study, we should attempt to determine the location where the village stood. We know that the bivouac of the Montana Column on the night of June 26, was at the present site of Crow Agency, Montana, 8¾ miles north of Reno Hill. According to Colonel John Gibbon and Captain Henry B. Freeman, they resumed the march early in the morning of June 27, and after only three miles, they came in sight of a huge deserted village.[17]

---

[16]Libby, *Arikara Narrative*, pp. 109-10.

[17]Thomas B. Marquis, *Custer, Cavalry and Crows*, p. 67; McClernand, *With the Indian and the Buffalo*, p. 59; Overfield, *Little Big Horn, 1876*, p. 84; Freeman Diary, Godfrey Family Papers.

The best mileage information is provided by Lieutenant William L. English, Seventh Infantry, who may have computed his figures from the actual odometer readings. According to Lieutenant English, the column came to the outskirts of the village after marching five miles. They subsequently went into camp below Reno Hill after logging a daily total of 8.76 miles. His diary reveals further that on June 28, they marched back on their trail and camped just below (north) where the village had stood, logging 4.65 miles.[18]

From the figures recorded by Lieutenant English, we should be able to locate the perimeters of the Indian village. We know that on June 27, the Montana column camped about a mile southeast of present Garryowen, on the flats west of the river, across from Reno Hill. We also know that the present Garryowen railroad station marked the southern end of the great village. By measuring a linear distance of 3¾ miles from the camp across from Reno Hill, we are able to compute the size of the village, which started at Garryowen and ended nearly three miles farther north.[19]

The computed village perimeter of three miles included both the old village site of June 25, and the new one of June 26. Failure to understand this fact caused many contemporary observers and subsequent researchers to go astray in their estimates of the population size. The configurations of both camp layouts were noted by Lieutenant Charles F. Roe, who wrote:

> The village was laid out in the form of an enormous circle, and adjoining it a three-sided rectangle; by actual measurement by an engineer sergeant [Charles Becker], from the circle on one side to the far side of the rectangle on the other side was three miles. Around the main teepees were wickiups made of willows used as

---

[18]Lt. William L. English Diary, Walter Mason Camp Papers, Denver Public Library, Item 3.

[19]Marquis, *Custer, Cavalry and Crows*, p. 72.

temporary shelter by warriors. The teepee poles had been left standing, but all their skins were stripped off.[20]

After consulting both contemporary and modern maps, I am convinced that the Indian village extended northward as far as present Squaw Creek. This seasonal watercourse used to enter the Little Bighorn from the west, just below and across from the mouth of Deep Ravine. Squaw Creek was known to the Lakotas as Shavings Creek, which the women and children of the Oglalas and Cheyennes ascended upon Custer's appearance across the river.[21]

Evidence that the village extended this far north is provided by Colonel John Gibbon who visited Custer's battlefield on June 29. Leaving Custer Hill, Colonel Gibbon later described the route he and his orderly took:

> On leaving the battleground, we bore obliquely to the right, and making our way over the steep bluffs down to the river, near the mouth of the deep gulch mentioned as containing so many of our dead troopers, pushed our way through the brushwood of the river-bank, and, crossing the river at a shallow ford, entered the site of the Indian camp, where our working parties were still busy searching for, collecting, and destroying the Indian property, part of which was found concealed in the brush.
>
> Riding across the valley towards the bluffs, we passed the site of the two teepies [sic] filled with dead Indians, now a mass of charred remains, and approached a clump of small trees, in and near which the Indians had buried a number of their dead, the ponies slaughtered in their honor lying about the remains of their dead masters, now tumbled upon the ground from the destruction of the scaffolding by those human ghouls whose existence seems to be inseparable from a fighting force, *after* the fighting is over, and whose vandal acts painfully impress one with the conviction that in war barbarism stands upon a level only a little lower than our boasted modern civilization.

---

[20]Roe, "Custer's Last Battle," pp. 10-11.
[21]Hardorff, *Lakota Recollections of the Custer Fight*, p. 26.

> The bodies lay upon the ground, the hideous display of their
> mortal corruption contrasting strangely with the gay robes and tin-
> sel trappings with which they had been carefully, perhaps lovingly,
> decked.[22]

From Colonel Gibbon's description, we learn that the two
lodges so often spoken of stood probably south of Squaw
Creek and across from Deep Ravine, in the three-sided rec-
tangle mentioned by Lieutenant Edward McClernand. This
conclusion receives support not only from McClernand himself, but also from Sergeant Stanislas Roy, as both told Walter
Camp that the teepees stood opposite Crazy Horse Gully,
which is now known as Deep Ravine. Indirect confirmation
of Gibbon's observation is provided by Trumpeter John Martin who recalled seeing the two lodges, and added that "only
about 100 yards away on the river bank, there was a pile of
dead Indians under a tree, with blankets thrown over them."[23]

The burial site in the "clump of small trees" seen by
Colonel Gibbon was probably the same site described by
Martin as being on the bench of the river. It does not seem
beyond the realm of possibility that the bodies found at this
location were originally laid out in a funeral lodge. If so, there
may have been as many as three lodges left standing at the
northern end of the village, a fact so noted by Lieutenants
Roe and Thompson.[24]

The likelihood exists that the burial site on the bench was
visited by several soldiers of the Seventh Cavalry. One of
them, Private Francis J. Kennedy, later recalled seeing a sin-
gle lodge in this vicinity with seven or eight dead Indians.[25]
His recollection is corroborated by Private Theodore W.
Goldin who saw this same lodge earlier:

---

[22]Col. John Gibbon, *Gibbon on the Sioux Campaign of 1876*, pp. 41-42.
[23]Camp Manuscripts, IU, pp. 547, 678; Hammer, *Custer in '76*, p. 105.
[24]Roe, "Custer's Last Battle," p. 10; Hammer, *Custer in '76*, p. 248.
[25]Carroll, *A Seventh Cavalry Scrapbook*, p. 26.

With Lieuts. [George D.] Wallace and [Luther R.] Hare, I, with a small party of soldiers, visited the field on the forenoon of the 27th and discovered a teepee standing in the shelter of the timber pretty much out of sight and tightly closed. Curious to see what it contained, Lieut. Wallace slashed a hole in the side of it with his knife, and we were all scared stiff at the howls that came from inside, and lit out for our horses, only to be stopped by the laughter of the horse-holders who pointed back toward the teepee. On looking back we saw just outside the hole made by Wallace, an Indian dog, whose ear was bleeding and we decided that Wallace must have cut him, and that the howls that stampeded us were simply his protest against that sort of treatment. In the teepee were six or seven dead warriors, evidently chiefs or warriors of importance, as two or three had their war bonnets on.[26]

One of the better descriptions of the burial sites was given by Private William H. White of the Seventh Infantry. He was assigned to Lieutenant Gustavus C. Doane's detail to collect bedding material on June 27, to transport the wounded. According to White, he saw several lodges still standing, some of which were at a location two-and-a-half miles northwest of the Garryowen railroad station. White recalled that all of these teepees stood near the foot of the benches on the west side of the river, and east of the present U.S. Highway 87:[27]

The teepees left by the Indians standing intact contained dead bodies of warriors. In one of them five dead bodies were on the ground, laid out carefully with all their best costumings and favorite face paintings and personal belongings, according to the Indian custom. In another were three dead bodies likewise placed for their Indian "burial." I saw, besides these, seven scaffolds, on each of which was the dead body of a warrior...

We roughly tumbled the corpses around on the ground in the teepees, to get from them the buffalo robes and blankets wrapped about them. These were to be used for making beds and litter ham-

[26]Carroll, *The Benteen-Goldin Letters*, p. 45.
[27]Marquis, *Custer, Cavalry and Crows*, p. 72.

mocks for the wounded men with Reno. Incidently, we looked with great interest upon the fine costumes and the Indian implements and trinkets wrapped in with the dead warriors. With one of them we found a 50-calibre single-shot Sharps rifle, and with one or two others we found cap-and-ball revolvers. Of course, I believe that all of the warrior bodies that could be found were robbed of their wrappings as well as their buffalo-skin shelters, and it is likely that not many of their personal belongings were left with them.[28]

William H. White's observations of the seven burial scaffolds is corroborated by a *New York Sun* reporter who passed over the village ground in August of 1877:

At last we entered the old village, in attacking which Custer and his men fell. This temporary Indian camp was about four miles long, and a half mile wide, and located by the river side, upon a depressed table-land, considerably lower than the valley proper. Its borders are fringed with a thin growth of timber, which at one time extended all over the bottom, but the felling of trees by the Indians to secure bark for their ponies, left the central portion of the strip almost barren. At the southern end, we passed through a dense copse covering three or four acres... Beyond this, the ground presented a curious spectacle, teepee and medicine poles were as thick as they could stand, while camp equipage of every kind was scattered all around. One noticeable feature consisted of the great quantity of leggings lying about, and is explainable only by the presumption (amounting to almost positive knowledge) that the Indians discarded them for the clothing taken from the soldiery. Further down we saw six burial scaffolds, and beneath them, where they had fallen, the bones of as many Indians—the skull of one punctured by and containing a bullet.[29]

In his narrative account, William White also identified some of the officers referred to by Colonel Gibbon as "human ghouls"—unprincipled men, who ignored the conduct code of the officers corps, and who blatantly desecrated the Indian remains:

---

[28]Marquis, *Custer on the Little Bighorn*, p. 12.
[29]*New York Sun*, Aug. 21, 1877.

Souvenir-gathering became a part of our activities there. I do not recall anybody among us having taken a scalp, but each one of our group of civilized people appropriated something or other of the personal property. I noted that Lieutenant Doane, who was the officer in command of my special group, took two or more pairs of moccasins. Dr. Paulding, our Second Cavalry Surgeon, longed to possess a certain pair of moccasins beaded on the soles as well as all over the uppers, and which were laced on the feet of one of the dead bodies. He tugged at getting them off the feet, but they were a tight fit since his flesh was swollen, and the skin slipped when he took hold of a leg. Notwithstanding he was a doctor, the offensive odor and the repugnant situation in general caused him to quit his undertaking. Those bodies had been lying there through two days and nights of the warm summer weather...[30]

Not mentioned by William White is Captain Otho E. Michaelis who opened a sepulchered bundle and removed a rifle in a beaded gun case, and also took an eagle feather with colored ribbon from the deceased's scalplock. This hair adornment was stained with blood from a gunshot to the head, the stains still being visible many years later.[31]

Before summarizing the evidence, I would briefly like to discuss what is known as the Ball Scout. On the morning of June 28, Company H of the Second Cavalry, under command of Captain Edward Ball, commenced a reconnaissance along the trail made by the Indians when they left the valley. Ball followed this trail for some ten miles, which was found to run in a southerly direction, towards the Big Horn Mountains. Here the trail was seen to split, upon which Captain Ball returned to the Little Bighorn Valley.[32]

Much has been made of this reconnaissance, especially of alleged observations of numerous Indian dead, found along

[30]Marquis, *Custer on the Little Bighorn*, p. 12.
[31]John M. Carroll, "The Mystery of Custer's Last Battle Cyclorama Unravelled," (Little Big Horn Associates) *Research Review* (December, 1983):18.
[32]Alfred H. Terry, *The Terry Diary: Yellowstone Expedition of 1876*, p. 10.

the trail. It was first mentioned in Major Marcus A. Reno's *Official Report,* and also in the *New York Times* of July 8, 1876, which speaks of many Indian dead, secreted in ravines a great distance from the battlefield, among which were Sioux, Cheyennes and Arapahoes. Curiously, Captain Thomas McDougall reiterated this rumor, identifying Captain Ball as his source.[33]

There were others who had heard of this matter, among which Lieutenant Winfield S. Edgerly who thought that thirty or more bodies had been found by Ball during the scout. And then there is the story told by Private Dennis Lynch, who claims that members of Ball's command told him about finding many bodies in a coulee, but that they did not count the decomposing corpses due to the putrefying odor. However, another source claims there were as many as one hundred and fifty![34]

Strangely, to say the least, the official documents are silent on the subject of finding these alleged Indian dead. Although General Alfred H. Terry mentioned the Ball Scout and its results in a telegram, he fails to confirm the finding of any Indian bodies, a matter which, most certainly, would have been brought to his attention if factual. The same holds true for Colonel John Gibbon, who mentions Captain Ball in his *Official Report,* but he writes nothing about dead Indians found by his subordinate.[35]

This contradictory matter did not escape Walter M. Camp, who sought a clarifying answer from several members of the Montana Column. One of these was Private William Moran, Seventh Infantry, who disclaimed ever having heard

[33]Hammer, *Custer in '76,* p. 73.

[34]Edward C. Baily, "Echoes from Custer's Last Fight," *Military Affairs* (Winter, 1953):180; Hammer, *Custer in '76,* p. 139; Bruce R. Liddic, *I Buried Custer: The Diary of Pvt. Thomas W. Coleman, 7th U.S. Cavalry,* p. 136.

[35]Terry, *The Terry Diary,* p. 10; Overfield, *The Little Big Horn,* 1876, p. 86.

that "Ball's scout up the Little Bighorn [had] reported to have found Indian bodies in coulee." The same answer was repeated by General Edward J. McClernand, who told Camp that he never had heard that Ball found any dead Indians during the scout on June 28.[36]

What, then, are we to make of the "reported" Indian dead found by Captain Ball? Personally, I think the whole matter was a rumor, born from half-truths, innuendos and misconceptions. Ball probably did find some bodies along the trail, but these were most likely the scaffolded remains found in the village. I am equally certain he found the bodies near the mouth of Shoulder Blade Creek, purported to have been the remains of ten women and children.

Other than the bodies already mentioned, I do not believe that Captain Edward Ball found any dead Indians along the trail leading to the Big Horn Mountains. Indian sources are very positive that only three men died from the trauma of their wounds—two Lakotas on Wood Louse Creek, and one Cheyenne near the Powder River. I am certain, therefore, that the reports of numerous remote Indian dead were nothing more than a rumor, used by Major Marcus A. Reno to soften the embarrassing defeat of the glory-seeking Seventh.

---

[36]Camp Manuscripts, IU, pp. 362, 548.

The Red Horse Pictographs

Five years after his surrender to the Military at the Cheyenne River Agency in 1876, the Minneconjou Lakota Red Horse drew a series of forty-two pictographs in crayon colors to accompany his account of the custer Fight. The five drawings reproduced in this volume reflect Red Horse's conception of the Indian dead. Representing both the Lakota and the Cheyenne casualties, the drawings show a number of Dog Soldiers and a Shirt Wearer among the slain. Although Red Horse imagined the casualty count to be as high as sixty-four, the mortality rate among the severely wounded was considerably less than anticipated, the final dead count being only half that much. *Courtesy National Anthropological Archives, Smithsonian Institution.*

Pictograph No. 26

Pictograph No. 27

Pictograph No. 28

Pictograph No. 29

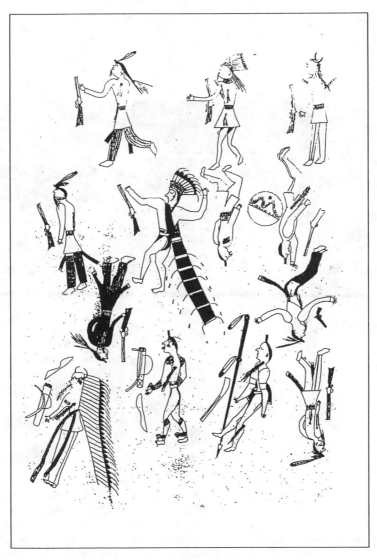

Pictograph No. 30

This group of seven elderly Lakotas includes six veterans who fought Custer at the Little Bighorn. Standing, left to right: Iron Hail, High Eagle, Iron Hawk, and Little Warrior; sitting, left to right: Comes Again, Pemmican, and John Sitting Bull (born 1884). This photo was taken in the Black Hills of South Dakota during September 1948, by an unknown artist. *Courtesy Custer Battlefield National Monument.*

CHAPTER SIX

Casualty Numbers and Indian Testimony

No sooner had the battle of the Little Bighorn ended, when speculation began about the number of casualties among the Indians. This matter was inevitably brought up during investigatory interviews, conducted by inquisitive whites, who had very little insight into the Indian frame of mind. Consequently, the information so obtained was subject to the Indian's degree of trust in the white man's motives. In addition, it was imperative that the latter procured and analyzed the evidence with an objective mind. More often than not, either one or both of these components were lacking, resulting in greatly exaggerated Indian casualty totals.

For the purpose of a statistical study, I compiled data for many years on the subject of Indian casualties. This data was primarily obtained from Hunkpapa and Oglala sources because their reservations were more accessible in the past to enquiring whites. This data is arranged according to the interview date it was obtained. To the best of my knowledge, the resulting compilation presents all of the pertinent data available, its base being broad enough to allow a balanced conclusion.

As early as 1876, the Blackfoot Lakota, Kill Eagle, told the Military that the Indians had sustained sixty-seven killed and six hundred wounded. He added that the Oglalas alone transported twenty-seven wounded on travoises and thirty-eight tied across ponies. Kill Eagle was an agency Indian, distrusted by the roaming tribes. It is possible, therefore, that Kill Eagle merely estimated these numbers, or, more likely, inflated these totals to satisfy the demanding whites.[1]

That same year, the Minneconjou, Red Horse, was questioned by Army Surgeon McChesney about the Indian dead. Red Horse disclosed that the casualties amounted to 136 dead and 160 wounded. It should be pointed out that these totals were obtained during lengthy interrogations, which may have resulted in some intentional distortions.[2]

The following year, 1877, the Oglala, Horned Horse, was interviewed at Camp Robinson by a Chicago newspaper correspondent. Horned Horse related that the Indian loss was fifty-eight killed, and over sixty wounded. However, the reporter was given the understanding that sixty percent of the wounded eventually died, which translates into an aggregate dead count of more than ninety. This interview was conducted only days after Horned Horse had surrendered, which fact may have had some bearing on his answers.[3]

In the same year, 1877, a number of Oglalas and Brules visited Custer Battlefield in the company of several generals and escort units of the Army. Classified as hostiles the previous year, they had now enlisted as U.S. Indian Scouts and explained to the military dignitaries that between thirty and

---

[1]*New York Herald*, Sept. 24, 1876.

[2]Graham, *The Custer Myth*, p. 60.

[3]*Chicago Times*, May 27, 1877.

forty Indians had been killed, and a very large number wounded.[4]

In 1879, the Hunkpapa, Little Knife, was approached by a reporter at Woody Mountain, Canada. Little Knife related that the Indian casualties on the battlefield amounted to thirty-two dead. In view of the Indian's unencumbered frame of mind, this total may well reflect the actual Indian fatalities, the number not distorted by distrust or other outside influences.[5]

Two years later, in 1881, the Hunkpapa, Crow King, told the Military that from thirty to fifty Indians were killed, and that a much greater number of wounded eventually died from their injuries. However, Crow King made this statement while he was a prisoner of war, a status which may have fostered a distortion to appease the whites.[6]

In the same year, 1881, the Oglala, Low Dog, informed the same Military that thirty-eight Indians had died outright, and that a great many of the wounded passed away afterwards. He added that he had never been in a fight in which so many in proportion to the killed had been wounded. Although this ratio was probably true, his comment that "a great many" died afterwards, was quite likely another appeasement to the Military.[7]

One of the few Lakota women asked to comment on the dead, was the Hunkpapa, Pretty White Buffalo Woman. She stated in 1883, that the Indian loss was thirty killed, and that more than twice this number had been wounded. She told Phillip Wells, a mixed-blood Sioux interpreter, that the Lakota dead count was only twenty-two, but that the Hunkpapa alone had sustained fifteen or sixteen wounded.[8]

[4]Graham, *The Custer Myth*, p. 115.
[5]*Billings Gazette*, June 25, 1926.
[6]*Leavenworth Weekly Times*, Aug. 18, 1881.   [7]Ibid.
[8]St. Paul *Pioneer Press*, May 19, 1883; Thomas E. Odell, "Ninety-Six Years among the Indians...," *North Dakota History* (July, 1949):210.

In 1886, the Hunkpapa, Gall, was offered a large purse of money for an interview at Custer Battlefield. Gall stated that the Indian loss amounted to forty-three killed, including several women and children. He added that nearly as many died from wounds every day "while going up Lodge Pole Creek," a clear contrast to other evidence presented later.[9]

Another form of motivation was used in the case of the Hunkpapa, Rain in the Face, who was induced to talk through consumption of liquor. He told Thomas Kent in 1894, that the Indian loss amounted to only fourteen or sixteen killed. This number probably reflected the casualties among the Indians living on the northern reservations only, with whom Rain was better acquainted. His total probably did not include the Oglala and Cheyenne dead.[10]

In the same year, 1894, George Barlett opened a trading post on Pine Ridge Reservation and succeeded to gain the confidence of the Oglalas. Eventually, they told him about the Custer Fight, and as a result of this information he came to the belief that only thirty-six Indians had been killed. About the same time, up north, a U.S. Indian interpreter, Jirah Isham Allen, learned from the Cheyennes and Sioux that their loss was small, and amounted to thirty-seven killed and many wounded.[11]

In 1898, anthropologist George B. Grinnell interviewed the Northern Cheyennes, some of whom had participated in the Custer Fight. One of these, Soldier Wolf, told him that only six Cheyennes had been killed outright, and that some had been wounded, although not very many.[12]

---

[9]St. Paul *Pioneer Press*, July 18, 1886.

[10]Cyrus Townsend Brady, *Indian Fights and Fighters*, p. 291.

[11]George A. Barlett, "Custer's Last Fight," unpublished manuscript in Agnes W. Spring Collection.

[12]Soldier Wolf Interview on the Custer Fight, George B. Grinnell Manuscript, Braun Research Library, Los Angeles.

That same year, Grinnell met a very brave Cheyenne named Tall Bull. This man told Grinnell that he had charged up the slope of Custer Hill, but before he could reach the soldiers his pony dropped dead from the effects of seven bullet wounds. He added that only six Cheyennes had been killed in the fight, among which was his brother-in-law, Lame White Man.[13]

Also in 1898, Hamlin Garland visited the Northern Cheyennes to interview Two Moons about the Custer Fight. When asked about the Indian casualties, Two Moons replied that thirty-nine Sioux and seven Cheyennes had been killed, and that about one hundred Indians had been wounded.[14]

In 1906, a retired judge, Eli S. Ricker, was told by the Oglala, Fears Nothing, that the Indians lost twenty dead on the battlefield. He recalled that two more died later on Wood Louse Creek, and that the total of twenty-two killed was the actual dead count. This may be true as to the Lakota dead, but it does not include the Cheyenne fatalities.[15]

Ricker gained a different impression from Charles Clifford, who in the same year related to him hearsay information. Apparently, Clifford's source was the Oglala, Yellow Horse, who was overheard saying that eighty-three Indians had fallen in the fight, and that others "were dying from wounds for three weeks afterwards."[16]

Also in the same year, 1906, Ricker learned from Nicholas Ruleau that the Oglala, Red Hawk, had told him that three hundred Indians had been killed during the battle, and that two hundred more died from their wounds while moving back to the agencies. Very little needs to be said about these

[13]Tall Bull Interview on the Custer Fight, Grinnell Manuscript.
[14]Graham, *The Custer Myth*, p. 103.
[15]Respects (Fears) Nothing Interview, Eli S. Ricker Collection, Nebr. St. Hist. Soc.
[16]Charles Clifford Interview, Ricker Collection.

numbers, except that somebody was either very gullible, or showed a definite deficiency in placing decimal points.[17]

The following year, 1907, Ricker interviewed a revered Oglala *Wicasa Wakan* (Holy Man) named Horn Chips who told him that only thirty-two Indians had been killed. He added that quite a few were wounded, but that these men "pulled through." Still favorably impressed with Red Hawk's absurd numbers, Ricker commented in his notebook not to take great stock in the totals given by Horn Chips.[18]

It is true that Horn Chips was not present at the battle of the Little Bighorn, but it should be noted that he received his information from the renowned Oglala, Crazy Horse, to whom he was a spiritual advisor. Perhaps Ricker changed his conclusions about Horn Chips when he learned in 1907, from another Oglala, Flying Hawk, that the entire Indian loss, including the fatally wounded, did not exceed thirty.[19]

In the same year, 1907, Ricker was told by the Hunkpapa, Iron Hawk, that about nineteen Indians were killed during the battle. He added that others were wounded, but that he did not know how many. Apparently, Iron Hawk's total referred to the Lakota dead only, and does not seem to include the Cheyennes, with whom he was less acquainted.[20]

Also in 1907, Ricker interviewed the Minneconjou, Standing Bear, who made it very clear that he had personally seen twenty-four dead Indians. He added, however, that others had died from their wounds, but that he did not know how many.[21]

In 1909, Walter M. Camp was told by the Oglala, Lone

---

[17]Nicholas Ruleau Interview, Ricker Collection.
[18]Chips (Encouraging Bear) Interview, Ricker Collection.
[19]Flying Hawk Interview, Ricker Collection.
[20]Iron Hawk Interview, Ricker Collection.
[21]Standing Bear Interview, Ricker Collection. The Ricker interviews mentioned here have been published by Hardorff in *Lakota Recollections of the Custer Fight*.

Bear, that only thirty Indians were killed outright, and that five more died from their wounds. Camp was a very knowledgeable and diligent researcher whose efforts to obtain the historical truth knew no bounds.[22]

In the same year, 1909, William O. Taylor, a survivor from the Little Bighorn fight, received several letters from an educated Oglala named Corn. Asked about the Indian fatalities, Corn disclosed that only twenty-seven Indians were killed, twenty-one of which resulted from Custer's battle.[23]

In 1909, Joseph K. Dixon realized his life's dream of holding a grand council for representatives of the vanishing Indian tribes. Among those who attended was the Two Kettle Lakota, Runs the Enemy, who told Dixon that in his estimate only fifty Indians were killed, but that others had died from their wounds later.[24]

During 1910, Walter M. Camp interviewed two other Oglalas. One of these was Horn Chips, who reiterated to Camp what he had told Ricker, namely, that only about thirty Indians were killed. The second informant was the Oglala, He Dog, a tribal historian, who estimated the casualties between thirty and forty. He added that many more were wounded, but that only a few of these died later from their wounds.[25]

For the purpose of this study, one of the more important interviews took place in 1912, when Walter Camp met the Minneconjou, White Bull. He told Camp that the allied Indian loss was twenty-six dead, and he showed Camp a ledger which contained the names of the fatalities. He stated

---

[22]Lone Bear Interview, Walter Camp Collection, Custer Battlefield National Monument.

[23]Charlie Corn to William O. Taylor, Sept. 15, 1909, Camp Collection, CBNM.

[24]Dixon, *The Vanishing Race*, p. 179.

[25]Walter Camp Notes, BYU, p. 287.

further that only two Indians had died from the trauma of their wounds.[26]

In 1919, the Minneconjou, Feather Earring, gave an account of the Custer Fight to General Hugh L. Scott. During the conversation, Feather Earring told Scott that he still remembered the names of sixteen dead Lakotas, and he added that the number of wounded was terrible.[27]

One of the better known Cheyenne informants was Wooden Leg, who was met by Thomas B. Marquis in 1926. This chance meeting resulted in a long association, culminating in a biography of this Cheyenne. Wooden Leg told Marquis that the Indian casualties of the Custer Fight amounted to twenty-five Sioux and seven Cheyennes.[28]

In 1927, Marquis interviewed a number of Cheyennes, among which was Big Head Woman, the sister of Chief White Bull. Asked about the Indian dead, she told Marquis that the loss was twenty-four Sioux and seven Cheyennes, among which was her nephew Noisy Walking.[29]

In the same year, Marquis met a very old Cheyenne who was asked to relate his first impression of the whites. He told Marquis that the very first whites he had seen had come in wagons drawn by oxen, shouting something which sounded to him like "coodem." So for a while, he and others called the whites the Coodem People. Asked about the Custer Fight, the old man replied that the dead count was thirty, among which were seven Cheyennes.[30]

In 1930, several Hunkpapas related to Walter Campbell details about the Indian dead. One of the informants, One Bull, related that there was no dancing on the night of June

[26]Walter Camp Manuscripts, IU, pp. 336-37.
[27]Graham, *The Custer Myth*, p. 98.
[28]Marquis, *Wooden Leg*, p. 274.
[29]Marquis, *Custer on the Little Bighorn*, p. 40.
[30]Marquis, *Cheyenne and Sioux*, p. 35.

25, because the people were mourning the loss of thirty dead. This same reason was given by Little Soldier, except that his fatality total was fifty.[31]

During 1930, and again in 1932, the Minneconjou, White Bull, was also interviewed by Campbell who later wrote a stirring biography of this very brave Lakota man. White Bull told Campbell that the Indian loss was twenty-eight men, including the casualties sustained by the Cheyennes.[32]

In the early 1930s, Floyd S. Maine visited a Lakota friend on Pine Ridge Reservation. While there, Maine met an aged Lakota named White Buffalo, who told him that the Indian casualties of the Custer Battle resulted in a dead count of thirty.[33]

In 1936, the Hunkpapa, Little Soldier, was interviewed once more, this time by Joseph G. Masters. Little Soldier told him that the estimate was sixty-four killed, which is an upward revision of his earlier total given to Campbell. However, this higher total is corroborated by a brave Hunkpapa woman, Moving Robe, who participated in the Custer Fight. Better known as Mary Crawler, she told Frank Zahn that the Indian loss amounted to over sixty killed, among which were some women.[34]

In 1938, Robert Frazier was accorded an interview with a very aged Cheyenne named Weasel Bear. Being near death, the old man told Frazier that the Cheyenne had seven killed.[35]

This concludes the evidence from our data base, which is included in the appendix in an abbreviated form. Let us now

---

[31]One Bull Interview, and Little Soldier Interview, both in Campbell Collection, Box 104, File 6.
[32]White Bull Interviews (1930, and 1932).
[33]Maine, *Lone Eagle*, pp. 131-32.
[34]Masters, *Shadows Fall Across the Little Horn*, p. 49.
[35]Frazier and Robert Hunt, *I Fought With Custer*, p. 127.

focus on an objective interpretation of the evidence. If we eliminate the two low responses (which represents the Cheyenne casualties only) and do the same with the two high responses (which seem exaggerated), we are left with a range from fourteen to eighty-three casualties. This range is divided as follows so as to learn the grouping of responses.

Casualty Ranges	Response Frequency
less than 20:	3
from 20 to 29:	5
from 30 to 40:	19
from 41 to 60:	6
from 61 to 83:	3

From this table we learn that the range "30 to 40" has a density of nineteen responses, which equals fifty-three percent of all the witnesses. The other ranges amassed considerably less responses. From this finding we may conclude conservatively that most witnesses thought the Indian casualties to run from thirty to forty. Although these casualty numbers do not distinguish the sexes, we know from the foregoing text and from the appendices shown hereafter that they consisted of thirty-one males, six females, and probably four infants.

Appendices

APPENDIX A-I

LAKOTA CASUALTIES
THE KICKING BEAR ROSTER

Informant: Kicking Bear *(Mato Wanartako)*
Tribe: Oglala Lakota
Interviewer: Indian Agent
Location: Pine Ridge Agency
Date: Circa 1898
Source: Southwest Museum, Los Angeles

Name of Fatality	Tribe
1. Bear Horn	Hunkpapa
2. Black White Man	Oglala
3. Dog Back	Minneconjou
4. Elk Standing Alone	Sans Arc
5. Lone Dog	Sans Arc
6. Long Road	Sans Arc
7. Plenty Lice	Oglala
8. Red Face	Hunkpapa
9. Save Himself	unidentified
10. Standing Rabbit	unidentified
11. Swift Bear	Hunkpapa
12. White Bull	Hunkpapa
13. White Eagle	Oglala

Editorial note: Born in an Oglala camp in 1848, Kicking Bear was a tribal member of Big Road's band of *Oyukpe* Oglalas. He later married a niece of the Minneconjou, Big Foot, and achieved the status of a minor leader in that band. He is perhaps best known for his fanatical role in the Ghost Dance troubles. Kicking Bear may have been related to the Oglala, Crazy Horse, of whom he was a close associate in matters of war. Since Kicking Bear fought alongside the Oglalas in the Custer Fight, he may have had personal knowledge of the five Oglala dead. However, only three of the names on his list were identified as Oglalas, while two other names do not appear on the list of anyone else. This leads me to believe that Save Himself and Standing Rabbit were the nicknames of Yellow Hair and Young Skunk, who both were Oglalas. In the above roster, the tribal affiliations have been added for the convenience of the reader.

Appendix A-II

THE WHITE BULL ROSTER #1

Informant:	Slow White Bull *(Pte San Hunka)*
Tribe:	Minneconjou Lakota
Interviewer:	Walter M. Camp
Location:	Standing Rock Reservation
Date:	1912
Source:	Camp Manuscripts, Indiana University

Name of Fatality	Tribe	Fatality Location
1. Bad Yellow Hair	Oglala	Custer Fight
2. Bear Elk	Sans Arc	Custer Fight
3. Bear with Horns	Hunkpapa	Reno Fight: bottom
4. Cloud Man	Sans Arc	Custer Fight
5. Deed, or Act	Sans Arc	Killed at distance
6. Dog's Back Bone	Minneconjou	Reno Fight: hill
7. Dog with Horns	Minneconjou	Reno Fight: bottom
8. Elk Standing High	Sans Arc	Reno Fight: going up hill
9. Flying Charge	Siha Sapa	Reno Fight: bottom
10. Killed	Sans Arc	Custer Fight
11. Long Road	Sans Arc	Reno Fight: hill
12. One Dog	Sans Arc	Custer Fight
13. Plenty Lice	Oglala	Custer Fight
14. Rectum	Hunkpapa	Custer Fight
15. Swift Bear	Hunkpapa	Reno Fight: bottom
16. Three Bears	Minneconjou	Reno Fight: bottom
17. White Bull	Hunkpapa	Reno Fight: bottom
18. White Eagle	Oglala	Reno Fight: going up hill
19. Young Skunk	Oglala	Custer Fight

About 1892, or before, White Bull went to all the tribes and got names of killed. [He] took great pains to get it correct. Wrote it down in a book which I [Walter M. Camp] saw.

———

Editorial note: For a biography of this great Minneconjou, see Stanley Vestal (Walter Campbell), *Warpath, The True Story of the Fighting Sioux, Told in a Biography of Chief White Bull.* No matter how great his war exploits may have been, his achievement to learn to write in the Lakota language in 1879 seems an even greater accomplishment. Flying Charge, the individual listed as a Siha Sapa (Blackfoot) Lakota, was probably a Hunkpapa by birth who was known to others by a different name. A note in the Campbell Collection reveals that "Black Moon was *Kuwa Kiyapi,*" which means literally translated, "Chase Flying." Confirmed by other sources, Flying Charge was better known as Young Black Moon, one of three sons born to the Hunkpapa leader, Black Moon, who died at Standing Rock in 1888. This roster was published in Kenneth Hammer's, *Custer in '76.* However, Dr. Hammer's assistants mistook Camp's informant, White Bull, for the renowned leader of the Northern Cheyennes, whose name was also White Bull.

APPENDIX A-III

THE WHITE BULL ROSTER #2

Informant: Slow White Bull *(Pte San Hunka)*
Tribe: Minneconjou Lakota
Interviewer: Walter Campbell
Location: Cherry Creek, Cheyenne River Reservation
Date: 1930
Source: Walter Campbell Collection,
                  University of Oklahoma

Name of Fatality	Tribe	Fatality Location
1. Bad Light Hair	Oglala	Custer Fight
2. Bear with Horn	Sans Arc	Custer Fight
3. Chase by Owl	Two Kettle	Reno Fight: bottom
4. Cloud Man	Sans Arc	Custer Fight
5. Dog Back Bone	Minneconjou	Reno Fight: hill
6. Dog with Horn	Minneconjou	Reno Fight: bottom
7. Elk Bear	Sans Arc	Custer Fight
8. Elk Stand on Top	Sans Arc	Reno Fight: bottom
9. Hawk Man	Hunkpapa	Custer Fight
10. Kill Him	Sans Arc	Custer Fight
11. Lone Dog	Sans Arc	Custer Fight
12. Long Road	Sans Arc	Reno Fight: hill
13. Many Lice	Oglala	Custer Fight
14. Rectum	Hunkpapa	Custer Fight
15. Red Face	Hunkpapa	Custer Fight
16. Swift Bear	Hunkpapa	Reno Fight: bottom
17. Three Bears	Minneconjou	Reno Fight: bottom
18. White Bull	Hunkpapa	Reno Fight: bottom
19. White Eagle	Oglala	Reno Fight: bottom
20. Young Skunk	Oglala	Custer Fight

They brought all of them to camp and put all the dead in a big teepee. Some were buried other places. They did not take their dead with them to White Mountains [Big Horn Mountains], but two died on the way and they were buried where they died.

Editorial note: The two Lakotas who died later were Three Bears and Black White Man. The name of the latter is missing on the above roster. Bear with Horns is mistakenly identified as a Sans Arc, while in reality he was a Hunkpapa.

THE WHITE BULL ROSTER #3

Informant:	Slow White Bull *(Pte San Hunka)*
Tribe:	Minneconjou Lakota
Interviewer:	Walter Campbell
Location:	Cherry Creek, Cheyenne River Reservation
Date:	1932
Source:	Walter Campbell Collection, University of Oklahoma

Name of Fatality

1. Back Bone of Dog	12. Lone Dog
2. Bad Light Hair	13. Long Robe
3. Bear with Horn	14. Plenty Lice
4. Business*	15. Red Face
5. Chase by Owl	16. Standing Elk
6. Cloud Man	17. Swift Bear
7. Dog with Horn	18. Three Bear
8. Elk Bear	19. White Bull
9. Guts	20. White Eagle
10. Hawk Man	21. Young Skunk
11. Kill Him	

*Deeds (Wicohan), the first one to be shot.

———

Editorial note: The Lakota name *Canku Hanska* translates into Long Road, which English name may have sounded to the recorder as Long *Robe*. It was written down as such by Frederick Garder, who was Campbell's secretary, and who was known for his idiosyncratic spelling.

APPENDIX A-V

THE WHITE BUFFALO ROSTER

Informant: White Buffalo *(Tatanka Ska)*
Tribe: Unidentified
Interviewer: Floyd S. Maine
Location: Pine Ridge Reservation
Date: Circa 1935
Source: *Lone Eagle... The White Sioux*

Name of Fatality	Tribe
1. Bad Light Hair	Oglala
2. Bear with Horns	Hunkpapa
3. Chased by Owls	Two Kettle
4. Cloud Man	Sans Arc
5. Deeds	Sans Arc
6. Dog's Back Bone	Minneconjou
7. Dog with Horns	Minneconjou
8. Elk Bear	Sans Arc
9. Guts, or Open Belly	Hunkpapa
10. Hawk Man	Hunkpapa
11. Kills Him	Sans Arc
12. Lone Dog	Sans Arc
13. Long Robe	Sans Arc
14. Plenty Lice	Oglala
15. Red Face	Hunkpapa
16. Standing Elk	Sans Arc
17. Swift Bear	Hunkpapa
18. Three Bears	Minneconjou
19. White Buffalo Bull	Hunkpapa
20. White Eagle	Oglala
21. Young Black Moon	Hunkpapa
22. Young Skunk	Oglala
23. Black Fox	
24. Flying By	
25. Lefthanded Ice	

26. Mustache
27. Owns Red Horse
28. Swift Cloud
29. Young Bear

Some years ago, while on a visit to my old home on the Pine Ridge Reservation, I [Floyd S. Maine] spent some time at the ranch home of an old warrior friend, Spotted Rabbit, veteran of the Little Big Horn. Living in his home at the time was his uncle, Ta-tanka Ska (White Buffalo), then about eighty years old, also a veteran of the Custer battle. White Buffalo was sort of a historian of his tribe, and it was from him that I learned the names of the Sioux warriors killed by Custer's troops. The names on the original deerskin are sketched in Sioux picture writing and are the Oglala Dakota (Sioux) names. I have given a literal English translation to these twenty-nine names, and, as far as I know, this complete list has never been known outside the Sioux Nation and has never before been published… One died of his wounds a few days later, while on their hurried move to Canada, which would bring the total number of Sioux dead to thirty.

Editorial note: Although Maine assumed that White Buffalo's list included only Lakota casualties, in actuality the last seven entries are the Lakota names of Cheyenne fatalities. There are some striking similarities between the White Buffalo roster and the one compiled by Slow White Bull. It is a remarkable coincidence that some fifty years after the Custer fight, two lists with the same casualties are obtained from two informants with nearly identical names. From both rosters, the name Black White Man is missing. Both rosters include the seven Cheyennes, the names exactly the same, which rosters are shown separately in Appendix B. And on both rosters, the name of the Sans Arc, Long Road, is recorded by the phonetical name of Long Robe. Maine's Oglala friend probably told him that this uncle's name was White Bull which name Maine later may have translated back into Lakota, resulting in *Tatanka Ska*. Maine was also told that the old man was in his eighties, which was nearly identical to the age of Slow White Bull, who lived from 1849 until 1947. We also know that Slow White Bull had an adopted Oglala son, John Little Cloud, which may explain the former's periodic visits to Pine Ridge, the home of the Oglalas. There is, however, only one difference between the two rosters, which is the inclusion of Young Black Moon on White Buffalo's list, whose name is absent from Slow White Bull's. In view of all this evidence, I firmly believe that the identity of both old men are one and the same. I guess that Maine obtained his roster after Campbell's interview of 1932, because of the addition of Young Black Moon. In the above roster, the tribal affiliations have been added for the convenience of the reader.

APPENDIX A-VI

MISCELLANEOUS INFORMANTS

Name of Fatality	Location	Informant	Source
Back Bone of Dog	Reno Hill	White Bull	Campbell Collection
Bear Horn	Custer	Standing Bear	DeMallie, *Sixth Grandfather*
Big Design[1]	valley	He Dog	Blish, *Pict. Hist. Oglalas*
Black Moon	valley	Horned Horse	Finerty, *Warpath & Bivouac*
Black Moon	valley	unidentified	Sandoz, *Battle of the Little Bighorn*
Black Wasichu[2]	Wood Louse	Black Elk	DeMallie, *Sixth Grandfather*
Breech Cloth	Reno Hill	Old Bull	Campbell Collection
Business[3]	Reno Creek	White Bull	Campbell Collection
Deeds	west bank	One Bull	Campbell Collection
Dog's Back Bone	not given	Flying By	Camp Notes
Dog's Back Bone	not given	Takes Horses	Camp Notes
Dog's Back	Reno Hill	Old Bull	Campbell Collection
Eagle Hat[4]	Reno Hill	Flying By	Camp Notes
Elk Stands Above	hill ascent	He Dog	Blish, *Pict. Hist. of the Oglala Sioux*
High Eagle[5]	valley	unidentified	Sandoz, *Battle of the Little Bighorn*
High Elk	valley	Kill Eagle	*New York Herald*
Large Wound w. Guts[6]	valley	He Dog	Blish, *Pict. Hist. of the Oglala Sioux*
Long Road	Reno Hill	One Bull	Camp Notes
One Dog	not given	Hollow Horn Bear	Hardorff, *Lakota Recollections*
One Hawk[7]	Reno Creek	Mary Crawler	Campbell Collection

Name of Fatality	Location	Informant	Source
Plenty Lice	not given	Julia Face	Hardorff, *Lakota Recollections*
Three Bears	Wood Louse	Black Elk	DeMallie, *The Sixth Grandfather*
Two Bears[8]	Reno Creek	Feather Earring	Graham, *The Custer Myth*

[1] Since the informant himself was an Oglala, Big Design was probably a nickname for one of his five slain tribesmen.

[2] *Wasichu* is Lakota for "white man" which, with its adjective, identifies the Oglala known as Black White Man.

[3] The name Business is an English deviation of the Lakota word *Wicob'an*, which translates into Deeds.

[4] Eagle Hat is very probably another name for Long Road, because Camp's informant added that this individual was slain about 75 feet from Benteen's line.

[5] The tribal affiliation of High Eagle is not known; however, since most of the contacts of Sandoz lived on Pine Ridge, I assume that he may have been one of the five slain Oglalas.

[6] Large Wound with Guts is the Oglala known to others by the abbreviated name of Open Belly, Guts, or Rectum.

[7] One Hawk is very likely the formal name of the young Sans Arc known to others as Deeds.

[8] Feather Earring explained that Two Bears was a young Sans Arc who was killed by Reno scouts while looking for ponies. Undoubtedly, Two Bears was yet another name for the boy called Deeds.

APPENDIX A-VII

THE MILLER ROSTER

Informants: White Bull, One Bull, Kills Alive, Feather
Earring, Black Elk, Iron Hail, High Eagle, Iron
Hawk, Eagle Bear, and White Cow Bull
Tribe: unidentified
Interviewer: David Humphreys Miller
Date: 1935-1956
Source: *Custer's Fall: The Indian Side of the Story*

Name of Fatality	Tribe	Fatality Location
1. Bad Light Hair	Oglala	Custer Fight
2. Black White Man	Oglala	Custer Fight
3. Chased by Owls	Two Kettle	valley
4. Cloud Man	Sans Arc	Custer Fight
5. Elk Bear	Sans Arc	Custer Fight
6. Hawk Man	Hunkpapa	Reno Hill
7. High Horse	Minneconjou	Custer Fight
8. Kills Him	Sans Arc	Custer Fight
9. Long Dog	Sans Arc	Custer Fight
10. Long Elk	Minneconjou	Custer Fight
11. Long Road	Hunkpapa	valley
12. Long Robe	Sans Arc	Reno Hill
13. Plenty Lice	Oglala	Custer Fight
14. Rectum	Hunkpapa	Custer Fight
15. Red Face	Hunkpapa	Custer Fight
16. Standing Elk	Sans Arc	valley
17. Swift Bear	Hunkpapa	valley
18. Two Bears	Sans Arc	valley
19. White Buffalo	Hunkpapa	valley
20. White Eagle	Oglala	valley
21. Young Skunk	Oglala	Custer Fight

Editorial note: After reading Miller's publication in 1957, Walter
Campbell wrote a friend that "a good deal of it seems to be lifted from my

books, and that a good deal of the rest of it is unreliable." There may be
some justification for Campbell's indignation, because on Miller's roster
appears the name Long Robe instead of Long Road, which repeats an
error made by Campbell in both of his publications. In addition, Miller
lists a Long Dog, which repeats another Campbell error, although the
latter's field notes clearly show the name as *Lone* Dog. There are other
inconsistencies in Miller's list. Although he describes the death of Deeds
in novelized detail, Miller fails to include the young man's name in his
casualty list. And instead of Three Bears, Miller lists a Two Bears, a name
used by the Minneconjou, Feather Earring, in 1919 to describe Deeds to
General Scott, which interview was published in the *Custer Myth*. Since
Miller professed to be fluent in Lakota and had mastered the Plains sign
language, errors such as the ones described should not and would not
have happened, unless Miller embellished on the truth. There are other
errors, chief of which is his confusion with the Cheyenne casualties,
which subject will be brought up later. Miller did a creditable job in syn-
thesizing the Indian accounts. Unfortunately, Miller ignores professional
courtesy by not giving credit to the many published sources and their
authors, from which he "borrowed" so liberally.

CHEYENNE CASUALTIES
LAKOTA NAMES

Informant	Slow White Bull	Slow White Bull	Slow White Bull	White Buffalo
Tribe	Minneconjou	Minneconjou	Minneconjou	unidentified
Interviewer	Walter M. Camp	Walter S. Campbell	Walter S. Campbell	Floyd S. Maine
Location	Standing Rock	Cheyenne River	Cheyenne River	Pine Ridge
Date	1912	1930	1932	Circa 1935
Source	Camp Manuscripts Indiana University	Campbell Collection University of OK	Campbell Collection University of OK	*Lone Eagle*
FATALITIES				
1	Black Coyote	Black Coyote	Black Fox	Black Fox
2	Flying By	Flying By	Flying By	Flying By
3	Left Hand	Left Hander*	Left-Handed Ice	Lefthanded Ice
4	Full Beard	Bearded Man	Mustache	Mustache
5	Has Sorrel Horse	Owns Red Horse	Owns Red Horse	Owns Red Horse
6	Swift Cloud	Swift Cloud	Swift Cloud	Swift Cloud
7	Young Bear	unknown	Young Bear	Young Bear
		*Chief Ice's son		

APPENDIX B-II

CHEYENNE NAMES

	Brave Bear	Wooden Leg	Big Head Woman	Lone Bear
Informant	Brave Bear	Wooden Leg	Big Head Woman	Lone Bear
Tribe	Cheyenne	Cheyenne	Cheyenne	Cheyenne
Interviewer	George Bent	Thomas B. Marquis	Thomas B. Marquis	Floyd S. Maine
Location	So. Cheyenne Res.	No. Cheyenne Res.	No. Cheyenne Res.	No. Cheyenne Res.
Date	1916	1920s	1927	Circa 1935
Source	William R. Coe Coll. Yale University	*Wooden Leg*	*Custer on the Little BH*	*Lone Eagle*
FATALITIES				
1	Old Man	Hump Nose	Hump	Hump Nose
2	Loose Bones	Limber Bones		Limber Bones
3	Noisy Walking	Noisy Walking	Noisy Walking	Noisy Walking
4	Lame White Man*	Lame White Man	Lame White Man	Lame White Man
5	Open Belly	Open Belly	unknown, d. later	
6		Whirlwind	Whirlwind	Whirlwind
7	Black Bear**	Black Bear		Black Bear

*aka Crazy Wolf
**aka Cripple Hand

	Stands in Timber	Stands in Timber	Unidentified	
Informant				
Tribe	Cheyenne	Cheyenne	Cheyenne	
Interviewer	Margot Liberty	Peter J. Powell	David H. Miller	
Location	No. Cheyenne Res.	No. Cheyenne Res.	unidentified	
Date	Circa 1956	1960s	not given	
Source	*Cheyenne Memories*	*Sweet Medicine*	*Custer's Fall*	
FATALITIES				
1	Roman Nose	Roman Nose	Hump Nose	
2	Limber Bones	Limber Bones	Limber Bones	
3	Noisy Walking	Noisy Walking	Noisy Walking	
4	Lame White Man	Lame White Man	Lame White Man	
5	Cut Belly	Cut Belly		
6	Little Whirlwind	Little Whirlwind	Whirlwind	
7	Closed Hand	Closed Hand	Black Bear	
			Black Cloud	Bearded Man
			Flying By	Owns Red Horse
			Left Hand	Swift Cloud

Editorial note: The last six names on Miller's roster are Lakota names of Cheyenne casualties, whose Cheyenne names Miller already had listed. It is rather peculiar, therefore, that Miller claims he obtained this information from his Cheyenne informants, especially since Miller professed to be fluent in the Cheyenne language. Comparison of Miller's roster with that of Walter Campbell reveals that the Lakota names of the six Cheyennes are one and the same. Furthermore, by listing Black Cloud, Miller unknowingly repeated a mistake made by Campbell, who accidentally transcribed the name of Black Coyote as Black Cloud, and then published the incorrect information.

APPENDIX C

CASUALTY NAMES IN LAKOTA

COMPOSITE LIST OF ENGLISH NAMES	WALTER M. CAMP'S PHONETICAL NAMES	PRESENT LAKOTA SPELLING
OGLALAS	OGALALLAS	OGLALA
1. Bad Light Hair	Pihin Zhi Shicha	Pehin Zi Śica
2. Black White Man		Waśicun Sapa
3. Many Lice	Tahea Ota	Hala Ota
4. White Eagle	Wambli Ska	Wanbli Ska
5. Young Skunk	Maka Chin Challa	Maka Cincala
MINNECONJOUS	MINNECONJOUS	MNIKOWOJU
6. Breech Cloth		Miyapahe
7. Dog with Horns	Sunka Heton	Śunka Heton
8. Dog's Back Bone	Sunka Chan Koha	Śunka Cankohan
9. Three Bears	Mato Yamni	Mato Yamni
TWO KETTLES		OOHENUNPA
10. Chased by Owls		Hinhan Okuwa
SANS ARCS	SANS ARCS	ITAZIPCO
11. Cloud Man	Mahcpiya Wichasta	Mahpiya Wicaśa
12. Deeds	Wichoka	Wicoh'an
13. Elk Bear	Mato Hehcahca	Mato Heh'aka
14. Long Road	Chanku Hanska	Canku Hanska
15. Lone Dog	Sunka Wanzila	Śunka Wanjila
16. Elk Stands Above	Hehcahca Wankal Nazin	Heh'aka Wankata Najin
17. Kills Him	Ktepila	Ktepila
HUNKPAPAS	HUNKPAPAS	HUNKPAPA
18. Bear with Horns	Mato Heton	Mato Heton
19. Guts	Tonzopsake	Taśupe
20. Hawk Man		Canśka Wicaśa
21. Red Face		Ite Luta
22. Swift Bear	Mato Oheanko	Mato Oh'anko
23. White Buffalo	Tatanka Ska	Tatanka Ska
24. Young Black Moon		Hanwi Sapa Cincala

CHEYENNES	CHEYENNES	ŚAHIYELA
25. Left Hand	Chatka	Catka
26. Has Sorrel Horse	Sunka Sha Yuha	Śunk'śa Yuha
27. Young Bear	Mato Chin Challa	Mato Cincala
28. Full Beard	Putihin Shina	Putinhin Śina
29. Flying By	Kinyan Hiyaye	Kinyan Hiyaye
30. Black Coyote	Shungomanitu Sapa	Śunk'manitu Sapa
31. Swift Cloud	Mahcpiya Oheanko	Mahpiya Oh'anko

ś = sh   h́ = guttural   ' as in h', k' = glottal stop

Editorial note: This roster in the Lakota language was taken from Walter M. Camp's handwritten notes in 1912, which are presently housed at the Indiana University. Although these notes were transcribed and published in *Custer in '76*, lack of familiarity with both Camp's handwriting and the Lakota language caused many errors in the roster's publication.

CASUALTY TABULATION
BY TRIBAL AFFILIATION

INFORMANT	TRIBE	YEAR	OG	MC	TK	SA	HP	BF	CH	OTHER
Kicking Bear	OG	1898	5	1		3	4			
Slow White Bull	MC	1912	4	3		7	4	1	7	
Lone Man[1]	HP	1912		3		6	7			
Flying By[2]	MC	1912		4						
Wooden Leg	CH	1920s	3	3		4	7		7	8
Slow White Bull	MC	1930	5*	3	1	6	6		7	
Slow White Bull[3]	MC	1932	5*	3	1	7	6		7	
White Buffalo		1935	5*	3	1	7	7		7	
Composite List			5	4	1	7	7		7	
*includes Black White Man										

[1]Source: Walter Camp Manuscripts, IU
[2]Ibid.
[3]Slow White Bull's figures are corroborated by Kicking Bear, Lone Man, and Flying By who each provided casualty totals for their own tribe. These independent numbers tend to reinforce the accuracy of the low dead count of 31 males.

ABBREVIATIONS FOR APPENDICES D AND E.
   OG = Oglalas; MC = Minneconjous; TK = Two Kettles; SA = Sans Arcs;
   HP = Hunkpapa; BF = Blackfoot; CH = Cheyenne

APPENDIX E

A CASUALTY TABULATION

INFORMANT	TRIBE	DATE OF INTERVW	KILLED	WOUNDED
Kill Eagle	BF	1876	67	600
Red Horse	MC	1876	136	160
Horned Horse	OG	1877	58	60+
Oglalas & Brules		1877	30-40	
Wm. Clark's Oglalas		1877	40	a large number
Little Knife	HP	1879	32	
Crow King	HP	1881	30-50	a large number
Low Dog	OG	1881	38	a great many died ltr
Pretty White Buffalo	HP	1883	30	60+
Gall	HP	1886	43	nearly as many died daily
Rain in the Face	HP	1894	14-16	
Barlett's Oglalas			36	
Two Moons	CH	1898	39+7 CH	100
Tall Bull	CH	1898	6 CH	
Fears Nothing	OG	1906	20+2 later	
Yellow Horse	OG	1906	83	others were dying for 3 wks.
Austin Red Hawk	OG	1906	300	200 died afterwards
Horn Chips	OG	1907	32	many, but recovered
Flying Hawk	OG	1907	30	
Iron Hawk	HP	1907	19	
Standing Bear	MC	1907	24	
Lone Bear	OG	1909	30+5 later	
Charlie Corn	OG	1909	27	
Runs the Enemy	TK	1909	50	others died a short time later
Horn Chips	OG	1910	30	
He Dog	OG	1910	30-40	many, only a few died
White Bull	MC	1912	26+2 later	
Feather Earring	MC	1919	16	a terrible number
Big Head Woman	CH	1927	24+7 CH	
Old Cheyenne	CH	1927	23+7 CH	
Wooden Leg	CH	1928	30+2 later	
One Bull	HP	1930	30	
Little Soldier	HP	1930	50	
Moving Robe	HP	1931	60	

White Bull	MC	1932	28	
White Buffalo		1935	30	
Little Soldier	HP	1936	64	
Weasel Bear	CH	1938	7 CH	

Bibliography
and
Index

Bibliography

Archival Sources

Billings, Montana. Billings Public Library. Billings Clipping File.

Bloomington, Indiana. Univ. of Indiana Library. Manuscripts Div. Robert S. Ellison Collection: Walter M. Camp Manuscripts.

Carlisle Barracks, Pennsylvania. Army War College Library. Research Collection: Edward S. Godfrey Family Papers.

Crow Agency, Montana. Custer Battlefield National Monument. Walter M. Camp Collection; Elizabeth B. Custer Collection. (CBNM)

Denver, Colorado. Denver Public Library. Western History Div. Robert S. Ellison Collection: Walter Mason Camp Papers.

Laramie, Wyoming. Univ. of Wyoming Library. Special Collections: Agnes W. Spring Collection.

Lincoln, Nebraska. Nebraska State Hist. Soc: Eli S. Ricker Collection.

Los Angeles. Southwest Museum, Braun Research Library. Manuscript Collections: George B. Grinnell Manuscript.

Norman, Oklahoma. Univ. of Oklahoma Library. Western History Collection: Walter S. Campbell Collection.

Provo, Utah. Brigham Young Univ. Library. Manuscripts Division: Walter Mason Camp Manuscripts.

Washington, D.C. Library of Congress. Manuscripts Division: Edward Settle Godfrey Papers.

Washington, D.C. Smithsonian Inst. National Anthropological Archives: Hugh L. Scott Collection.

West Point. Military Academy Library. Special Collections: John G. Bourke Diaries.

Printed Sources—Books

Blish, Helen H. *A Pictographic History of the Oglala Sioux.* Lincoln: Univ. of Nebr. Press, 1967.

Boyes, William. *Surgeon's Diary.* Washington, D.C.: South Capitol Press, 1974.

Brady, Cyrus Townsend. *Indian Fights and Fighters.* Lincoln: Univ. of Nebr. Press, 1971.

Brininstool, E.A. *Troopers With Custer.* New York: Bonanza Books, 1952.

Brown, Jesse and A.M. Willard. *The Black Hills Trails.* Rapid City: Rapid City Journal Co., 1924.

Burdick, Usher L. *Tales from the Buffalo Land.* Baltimore: Wirth Brothers, 1940.

Carroll, John M. *The Benteen-Goldin Letters on Custer and His Last Battle.* New York: Liverwright, 1974.

_____. *The Gibson and Edgerly Narratives.* Bryan, TX: privately printed, 1979.

_____. *A Seventh Cavalry Scrapbook, #10.* Bryan, TX: 1978.

Coffeen, Herbert. *The Custer Battle Book.* New York: Carlton Press, 1964.

DeMallie, Raymond J. *The Sixth Grandfather: Black Elk's Teachings Given to John G. Neihardt.* Lincoln: Univ. of Nebr. Press, 1984.

Dixon, Joseph K. *The Vanishing Race.* New York: Bonanza Books, 1975.

Finerty, John F. *War-path and Bivouac, or the Conquest of the Sioux.* Norman: Univ. of Okla. Press, 1961.

Gibbon, Col. John. *Gibbon on the Sioux Campaign of 1876.* Bellevue, NB: Old Army Press, 1970.

Graham, W.A. *The Custer Myth: A Source Book of Custeriana.* New York: Bonanza Books, 1953.

_____. *Abstract of the Official Record of the Reno Court of Inquiry.* Harrisburg, PA: Stackpole, 1954.

Grinnell, George B. *The Fighting Cheyennes.* Norman: Univ. of Okla. Press, 1956.

Hammer, Kenneth. *Custer in '76: Walter Camp's Notes on the Custer Fight.* Provo: Brigham Young Univ. Press, 1976.

Hardorff, Richard G. *Markers, Artifacts and Indian Testimony: Preliminary Findings on the Custer Battle.* Short Hills, NJ: Don Horn Publications, 1985.

_____. *The Custer Battle Casualties: Burials, Exhumations, and Reinterments.* El Segundo, CA: Richard Upton and Sons, 1989.

_____. *Lakota Recollections of the Custer Fight: New Sources of Indian-Military History.* Spokane, WA: Arthur H. Clark Co., 1991.

Hassrick, Royal B. *The Sioux: Life and Customs of a Warrior Society.* Norman: Univ. of Okla. Press, 1964.

Hunt, Frazier and Robert. *I Fought With Custer.* New York: Charles Scribner's, 1947.

Libby, Orin G. *The Arikara Narrative of the Campaign against the Hostile Dakotas, June, 1876.* New York: Sol Lewis, 1973.

Liddic, Bruce. *I Buried Custer: The Diary of Pvt. Thomas W. Coleman, 7th U.S. Cavalry.* College Station, TX: Creative Publishing Co., 1979.

Maine, Floyd Shuster. *Lone Eagle... The White Sioux.* Albuquerque: Univ. of New Mex. Press, 1956.

Marquis, Thomas B. *Wooden Leg.* Lincoln: Univ. of Nebr. Press, 1962.

_____. *Custer on the Little Bighorn.* Lodi, CA: End-Kian Publishing, 1971.

_____. *Sioux and Cheyennes.* Stockton, CA: Univ. of Pacific Press, 1973.

_____. *Custer, Cavalry and Crows.* Ft. Collins, CO: Old Army Press, 1975.

_____. *Keep the Last Bullet for Yourself.* New York: Two Continents Publishing Co., 1976.

Masters, Joseph G. *Shadows Fall across the Little Horn.* Laramie: Univ. of Wyo. Press, 1951.

McClernand, Edward J. *With the Indian and the Buffalo in Montana, 1870-1878.* Glendale: Arthur H. Clark Co., 1969.

McLaughlin, James. *My Friend the Indian.* Seattle: Superior Publishing, 1970.

Miller, David H. *Custer's Fall: The Indian Side of the Story.* Lincoln: Univ. of Nebr. Press, 1985.

Overfield, Loyd J., II. *The Little Big Horn, 1876: The Official Communications, Documents and Reports.* Glendale: Arthur H. Clark Co., 1971.

Powell, Peter J. *Sweet Medicine,* Vol. II. Norman: Univ. of Okla. Press, 1969.

[Ricky, Don]. *The Entrenchment Trail.* Billings, MT: Western Litho, 1969.

Roe, Gen. Charles F. "Custer's Last Battle," reprinted in *Custer Engages the Hostiles.* Ft. Collins, CO: Old Army Press, n.d.

Sandoz, Mari. *The Battle of the Little Bighorn.* Phila., 1966.

Stewart, Edgar I. *Custer's Luck.* Norman: Univ. of Okla. Press, 1955.

Stands in Timber, John and Margot Liberty. *Cheyenne Memories.* Lincoln: Univ. of Nebr. Press, 1972.

Terry, Gen. Alfred H. *The Terry Diary: Yellowstone Expedition of 1876.* Bellevue, NE: Old Army Press, 1970.

Upton, Richard. *Fort Custer on the Big Horn, 1877-1898.* Glendale: Arthur H. Clark Co., 1973.

Utley, Robert M. *The Reno Court of Inquiry: The Chicago Times Account.* Ft. Collins, CO: Old Army Press, 1972.

Vestal, Stanley. *Sitting Bull, Champion of the Sioux.* Boston: Houghton Mifflin, 1932.

_____. *Warpath: The True Story of the Fighting Sioux Told in a Biography of Chief White Bull.* Boston: Houghton Mifflin, 1934.

Wagner, Glendolin D. *Old Neutriment.* New York: Sol Lewis, 1973.

Weibert, Henry and Don. *Sixty-six Years in Custer's Shadow.* Billings, MT: Falcon Press, 1985.

Wheeler, Col. Homer W. *Buffalo Days.* Indianapolis: Bobbs-Merrill, 1925.

Yost, Nelly Snyder. *Boss Cowman: The Recollections of Ed Lemmon, 1857-1946.* Lincoln: Univ. of Nebr. Press, 1969.

Printed Sources—Articles

Baily, Edward C. "Echoes from Custer's Last Fight." *Military Affairs* (Winter 1953).

Buecker, Thomas S. "A Surgeon on the Little Big Horn." *Montana, the Magazine of Western History* (Autumn 1982).

Carroll, John M. "The Mystery of Custer's Last Battle Cyclorama Unravelled." (Little Big Horn Associates) *Research Review* (Dec. 1983).

Eastman, Charles H. "The Story of the Little Big Horn." *Chautauquan* (July 1900).

Hardorff, Richard G. "Custer's Trail to Wolf Mountains: A Reevaluation of Evidence." *Custer and His Times: Book Two.* Fort Worth, TX: Little Big Horn Associates, 1984.

Kanipe, Daniel C. "A New Story of Custer's Last Battle." *Contributions to the Historical Society of Montana.* Vol. IV (1903).

Odell, Thomas E. "Ninety-Six Years among the Indians…" *North Dakota History* (July 1948).

Peterson, Francis Y. "Dewey Iron Hail." *Frontier Times* (Fall 1961).

Newspapers

Billings Gazette, 1926, 1927
Chicago Times, 1877
Chicago Tribune, 1877
Leavenworth Weekly Times, 1881
New York Herald, 1876
New York Sun, 1877
St. Paul *Pioneer Press,* 1883, 1886

Index